HIDCOTE MANOR GARDEN

Gloucestershire

Anna Pavord

THE NATIONAL TRUST

Acknowledgements

I am most grateful to Oliver Garnett for suggesting that I should write this book. He has been a most scrupulous editor. I am also indebted to John Sales, the Trust's Gardens Adviser, who has provided valuable help. For detailed information on the plants at Hidcote, I must hank the dedicated team that looks after the garden: Paul Nicholls, Peter Dennis, David Owen, Philip Bowell, Geoffrey Fermor, Jon Heath and Ben Greenhalf. The extracts from James Lees-Milne's diaries are quoted by kind permission of the author.

Anna Pavord

First published in Great Britain in 1993 by the National Trust
© 1993 The National Trust
Registered charity number 205846
Reprinted 1995, 1997, 1998, 2000, 2001, 2002, 2003
ISBN 0 7078 0166 4

Designed by James Shurmer

Phototypeset in Monotype Bembo Series 270
by SPAN Graphics Limited, Crawley, West Sussex (9010)

Print managed by Centurion Press Ltd (BAS)
for the National Trust (Enterprises) Ltd,
36 Queen Anne's Gate, London SW1H 9AS

CONTENTS

INTRODUCTION

Too little is known about Lawrence Waterbury Johnston, who made the garden at Hidcote. He left no diaries and few letters, and wrote no articles about his grand creation, the product of 40 years work. No plans of work in progress or of the finished design have ever come to light. No lists of plants seem to have been made. Unlike most plantsmen of his day, he was not active in the powerful mafia of the Royal Horticultural Society. The few photographs that survive show a fair, sad-eyed little man, usually accompanied by dogs, at first springer spaniels, later dachshunds. One photograph survives of his formidable American mother, Gertrude Winthrop, who bought Hidcote at auction from a Mr John Tucker on 2 July 1907. The property included farmland of nearly 300 acres, a good farmhouse, mostly of the seventeenth century, but refronted in the eighteenth, farm buildings, grouped round a yard, and ten cottages – the whole of the hamlet of Hidcote Bartrim.

When the twice-widowed Mrs Winthrop arrived in Gloucestershire with Johnston, the only surviving son of her first marriage, he was already 36. For the first twenty years of his life he seems to have been part of that rootless, peripatetic band of cultured Americans whom Henry James brought to life so vividly in his novels of the period.

For four years in the 1890s, Johnston was at a crammer in Little Shelford in Cambridgeshire, and in 1894 went up to Trinity College, Cambridge. Shortly after he got his degree, a second in history in 1897, he became a naturalized British citizen and went off to fight in the Boer War with a Northumbrian friend, George Savile Clayton. This was the start of a military career that spanned the next twenty years. He fought in the First World War as a Major in the Northumberland Hussars, was

(*Opposite*) The White Garden (June)

wounded at Hooge Château and finished the war as second-in-command of his regiment. After that, Hidcote was his chief preoccupation, together with his garden near Menton on the French Riviera, La Serre de la Madone ('The greenhouse of the Madonna'), which he acquired in the late 1920s.

Hidcote came to the National Trust in 1948, when Johnston departed permanently for his garden in France, where he lived, in frail health, for another ten years. It was an important acquisition, important not only because of its quality, but because this was the first property that the Trust acquired specifically on account of its garden. Here the Trust learned to garden, a story that is told in Chapter Four. In 1949, Hidcote's first open season, visitors numbered 1,160. Twenty years on the figure had leapt to more than 60,000. In 1989, after another twenty years, 125,000 visitors came to the garden and the figures are still rising.

The National Trust has now owned the garden at Hidcote for longer than Johnston himself did. During this period the garden has, inevitably, changed, particularly with respect to its plants. A garden, unlike a house, does not stand still. Age, however, only enhances the true essence of Johnston's achievement, which is to have created a garden where the brilliance of the design is matched only by the richness and diversity of the planting within it. He found a field, some beech trees and a cedar, and left a garden as intricately conceived as any house, a garden of corridors and rooms, furnished in every detail. For inspiration, he borrowed from Italy, from France, from the cottage gardens around him in Gloucestershire, from the gardens of his friends. Then he fused all these disparate elements into a creation that was uniquely his own. There are many lessons to be learned at Hidcote and it is because of Lawrence Johnston's generosity that we are all in a position to learn them.

CHAPTER ONE
THE EDWARDIAN GARDEN

In 1907, when Lawrence Johnston and his well-heeled mother, Gertrude Winthrop, came to Hidcote, Edward VII was more than half way through his short and hedonistic reign, income tax was a shilling in the pound, and servants still plentiful and cheap. For those with money, England was a most comfortable place to be.

The popular image of the age is one of house parties, picnics, extravagant dresses and mindless chatter. But this was also an age of ideas. Freud and the philosopher G. E. Moore published books that still influence the way we think today. Roger Fry's infamous Post-Impressionist exhibition at London's Grafton Galleries in 1910 left conservative critics choking with rage, but those reviled pictures now fetch record-breaking prices. And in Gloucestershire Lawrence Johnston started to make the garden that, more than any other in England, has influenced the way we garden today.

An extraordinary explosion of garden-making took place in the decade before the Black Hole of the Great War. There was plenty of new money, earned from mines and shipbuilding and shops, to be spent and plenty of garden designers, working in quite different styles, to spend it.

The age was dominated by the architect Sir Edwin Lutyens and the partnership he formed with the much older plantswoman and gardener Gertrude Jekyll. By the time that Johnston came to Hidcote, they had already collaborated on masterpieces such as Folly Farm in Berkshire (1906) and Hestercombe in Somerset (1904–9). And in 1902 Lutyens had also prepared garden plans for Mark Fenwick at Abbotswood in Gloucestershire, a neighbour who was later to become a close friend of Johnston. The magazine *Country Life*, then, as now, an important arbiter of style, was full of their work. Johnston could scarcely fail to have been aware of it.

But there is little at Hidcote that echoes the heavily architectural style of a typical Lutyens garden. There are no pergolas or terraces, none of the intricately paved and patterned paths that were a Lutyens trademark. Where Lutyens used stone and brick, Johnston employed yew and beech and grass, but in an architectural way. And there is not the obvious relationship between house and garden that characterises a Lutyens commission. The garden at Hidcote, lying chiefly to the west of the house, is curiously separate from it. None of the vistas connects with the house in the way that was axiomatic in a Lutyens design.

With some of the general principles of garden-making that Lutyens voiced in an address to the Architectural Association in April 1908, Johnston would have agreed: 'A garden scheme should have a backbone – a central idea beautifully phrased.' And later, 'The true adornment of a garden lies surely in its flowers and plants.' Both those are true of Hidcote, which has not one but two strong backbones to connect the separate incidents of the garden rooms. And the garden, even in Johnston's day, was never heavily ornamented with statues or urns or vases. Plants were always the chief *raison d'être*, and became increasingly important as Johnston's knowledge grew.

When you are confronted with a man such as Johnston, who left no documentary evidence behind him, it is impossible to say with certainty why he did things as he did. We can only guess at the influences that may have guided him in particular ways. He can scarcely have escaped the influence of Gertrude Jekyll, for instance, who was the most influential plantswoman of her day. By the time that Johnston settled at Hidcote, she had already been working for more than twenty years on her garden at Munstead Wood, Surrey. There were peonies, Michaelmas daisies, a rock garden, a spring garden and the famous herbaceous border, 200 feet of it, fourteen feet wide, backed by a sandstone wall.

Her theories on colour and rules for good planting schemes culminated in one of her most important books, *Colour in the Flower Garden*, published in 1908. Jekyll colour schemes depended on a careful crescendo of effect, as she explained, describing her borders at Munstead Wood:

At the two ends there is a groundwork of grey and glaucous foliage. With this, at the near or western end, there are flowers of pure blue, grey blue, white, palest yellow and palest pink; each colour partly in distinct masses and partly intergrouped. The colouring then passes through stronger yellows to orange and red. By the time the middle space of the border is reached the colour is strong and gorgeous.

Gertrude Jekyll's main border at Munstead in 1900; watercolour by Helen Allingham, reproduced from M. B. Huish's *Happy England* (1903)

This central explosion was provided by hollyhocks, scarlet dahlias and salvias.

This book must have been in Johnston's extensive library (500 books sold after his death for £7), together with a subsequent volume, *Gardens for Small Country Houses*, which Jekyll published in 1912 with Lawrence Weaver, architectural editor of *Country Life*. Did Johnston plan his red borders, fired by Jekyllian principles? Did he install a lion's mask waterspout in the entrance yard at Hidcote because Jekyll had one, her only ornament, at Munstead Wood? It is unlikely that the borrowing was as directly obvious as this (although Hidcote's wooden entrance gates, with semicircular heads pierced by vertical bars, were evidently a direct copy of those at Cleeve Prior, Evesham, illustrated on p.194 of the latter book). As Johnston may have been thinking vaguely of Lutyens when he planned the wide semicircular flights of steps made from roofing tiles set on edge in the Bathing Pool Garden, so Jekyll must have been in mind when he planted his first borders. But, like Jekyll, Johnston was a talented painter. Manipulating colour would have been a familiar concept.

Lutyens and Jekyll did not have the field entirely to themselves in those busy years. Italy was an important influence – on both sides of the Atlantic. It was evident of course in the novels of Henry James. It was evident in the numbers of books about Italian gardens which began to appear. The American landscape painter turned architect Charles Platt published *Italian Gardens* in 1894. Edith Wharton, a fellow American who was to become a neighbour of Johnston in France in the 1920s, brought out her influential *Italian Villas and their Gardens* in 1904. 'The inherent beauty of the Italian garden lies in the grouping of its parts,' she wrote, 'in the converging of the lines of its long ilex walks, the alternation of sunny open spaces with cool woodland shade, the proportion between terrace and bowling green, or between the height of a wall and the width of a path.'

Think of the Pillar Garden at Hidcote with its severely architectural lines of clipped yew trees. Think of the amazingly ambitious Long Walk reaching out towards the distant horizon. Think of the smooth circle of water in the Bathing Pool

The central alley in Harold Peto's Upper Garden at the Villa Maryland on the Riviera, photographed in 1910

Garden, the raised pool mirroring the strict clipped façade of the yew hedge. And of the ilexes that Johnston planted so liberally round Hidcote's acres. It is not difficult to sense an Italian influence at work.

There were plenty of other garden-makers in England extolling the virtues of the Italian style, but they were not making gardens like Hidcote. The most eclectic was Sir George Sitwell, who created important gardens at Renishaw in Derbyshire and Montegufoni in Tuscany, and who published his *Essay on the Making of Gardens*, the fruits of his own research in 200 Italian gardens, in 1909. Only an inconvenient lack of cash left Sir George's wildest dreams for Renishaw unrealised: the stone boat to decorate the lake, the fake Roman aqueduct to frame an important view. Like Harold Peto and other architect-gardeners heavily influenced by Italy, he worked with water, statues, vistas, hedges, evergreens. He was not very interested in flowers.

Nor was Peto, who, in one of his rare pieces of writing, described 'the entirely subordinate place' that, in his opinion, flowers should hold in any

garden scheme. Like Lutyens, he was an architect (for a while Lutyens was apprenticed in Peto's office) and his gardens depend even more heavily than Lutyens's on buildings and masonry for their effects. His masterpiece is his own garden at Iford, south-west of Bradford-on-Avon, Wiltshire. He bought it in the early 1900s and during the following 30 years transformed it into an extraordinary patch of Italy with *casitas* and loggias, fountains and colonnades, cloisters and patios. But Peto was also a gardener and without its mounds of clipped phillyrea, swags of wistaria, tubs of agapanthus and splayed fans of fig, Iford would be an arid place. Despite this, he was not a plantsman; Johnston was, and that remains the greatest difference between them. However, there were similarities in the way they led their lives: both of them were, at heart, solitary, with one foot in England, the other firmly planted on the shores of the Mediterranean. And there is a strong echo of Peto in the little *casita* that Johnston built in the small paved garden by the bathing pool. The wall is set with ancient carved fragments of stone and pottery. You can still see the traces of blue paint from the decorative fresco that Johnston painted here.

Muddy Hidcote may seem an odd place for cosmopolitan Americans such as Gertrude Winthrop and her son to have put down roots, but for Henry James Americans, the area was a magnet. James himself had already written a rave piece about nearby Broadway in the American *Harper's Magazine*. And then the popular American actress Mary Anderson, retiring in 1889 from several wildly successful seasons at Stratford, married a fellow American, Antonio de Navarro, and settled at Court Farm in Broadway. Like everyone else with money in this age of ease and leisure, she made a garden, calling in the painter Alfred Parsons to help.

Parsons was an Arts and Crafts man, a member of an informal but influential movement involving painters, architects, gardeners and craftsmen of all kinds. Its gardeners favoured a cottagey quality, old-fashioned flowers and traditional garden crafts such as topiary. There was no uniform style, but an atmosphere created with natural materials, old stone buildings enclosing small planted courtyards, clipped peacocks on top of bulging hedges, pleached limes, lilies, old roses, scent, romance. It is the style of the areas immediately around the house at Hidcote: the Old Garden, the Maple Garden (though not then growing maples) and the White Garden with its cosy topiary birds. In Johnston's time this garden had a stone sundial at the centre – a must in all Arts and Crafts gardens.

Parsons was head gardener to the Arts and Crafts crew but plenty of others believed in the same principles. In 1902 the architect and craftsman Charles Ashbee had led a small band of the faithful to Chipping Campden, only a few miles south of Hidcote, to create a utopian settlement of well-planned cottages and workshops. They laid out gardens and allotments and established a school of arts and crafts known as the Guild of Handicraft, but the project foundered for lack of cash.

If the Cotswolds was the centre of the Arts and Crafts movement, then Rodmarton Manor, between Cirencester and Tetbury in Gloucestershire, was the apogee of the style. House and garden were begun together in 1909, designed by the Cotswold architect Ernest Barnsley. The garden was laid out either side of a corridor running from west to east. There were plenty of yew hedges and, at the end, a wild garden screened with hornbeam. When Barnsley died, his son-in-law, a similarly minded architect, Norman Jewson, took over the practice. He had arrived in the Cotswolds on a sketching tour the same summer that Mrs Winthrop bought Hidcote and later repaired the Hidcote buildings.

For the closest parallels to the Hidcote garden, you have to go much further north or much further south, where, before Johnston started on his own creation, the Hon. Robert James at St Nicholas, Richmond in Yorkshire and the Arts and Crafts architect Herbert Kitchin at Compton End near Winchester in Hampshire, were both making rather different types of garden. Hidcote includes the best elements of both. Kitchin's garden, which he started in 1897, was made round a brick cottage with thatch pulled down like a tweed hat over the windows. A wide grass path runs from the garden porch with herbaceous borders either side. Next to these, in a separate yew-hedged enclosure, is a pool garden, surrounded by flower beds. Fat broody topiary hens, beautifully clipped, guard the corners of the beds. A formal arrangement of box-edged beds filled with flowers leads down to a small wild garden and beyond that a plain lawn and a familiar-looking little pavilion, soft red brick with a white painted door and tall thin windows. The roof is swept up into a pyramid. Kitchin worked at Lyegrove in Gloucestershire for Lady Westmorland in 1926 and was also in the area in the summer of 1908 when he sketched Pope's seat at Cirencester House. But exactly how those Hampshire red brick pavilions with swept-up roofs arrived at the top of the Hidcote Red Borders, nobody knows for sure.

Bobbie James, whose business was building warships at Barrow-in-Furness, started his magnificent garden, St Nicholas, in 1905. Like Hidcote, it relies on evergreen hedges, rather than walls, to divide the garden into a series of architectural compartments. He gardened on a grand scale with elegant double borders 18 feet wide contained within pleached hornbeam hedges that stretched for more than a hundred yards. There was a large rock garden, reached through a woodland planting of rhododendrons and azaleas, some good roses (including the climber 'Bobbie James'), and an outstanding collection of unusual trees and shrubs.

There was also a cottage garden – the only touch of Arts and Crafts.

James was a friend of Mark Fenwick from Abbotswood, Stow-on-the-Wold, a rigorous gardener. Presumably, it was through Fenwick that Johnston first met James. Plantsmanship was what he learned from gardeners such as these and this is an important element of the Hidcote style, entirely missing from Arts and Crafts gardens. Johnston taught himself to become a discerning judge of

plants. An Arts and Crafts gardener would plant lilac, preferably the common type, for the smell. Johnston would have wanted specific varieties of lilac (for instance, for the Circle), and then, as he got even more particular, only certain vegetatively propagated forms of those varieties. He forged links with discerning nurserymen such as Clarence Elliott at Moreton-in-Marsh and other collector-gardeners such as Sir George Holford at nearby Westonbirt. His name crops up in the visitors' book at Nymans in Sussex, a garden where plantsmanship, as practised by the Messels, was the driving force of a gardening coterie even more single-minded than the Gloucestershire crowd.

This was a good time for anyone interested in new plants, for they were flooding in from all corners of the globe, thanks to the efforts of plant hunters such as the Chipping Campden man Ernest Henry Wilson, Cherry Ingram and George Forrest. Johnston began to subscribe to plant-hunting expeditions, and, after the death of his mother in 1926, went on some plant-hunting trips himself. With Cherry Ingram and Reginald Cory (who had started his important garden at Dyffryn near Cardiff in 1906), Johnston went to South Africa and Tanganyika for four months in 1927. They collected several showy lobelias and, from Mount Kilimanjaro, a large-flowered hypericum (possibly the one now called 'Hidcote'). Johnston included his chauffeur and valet in the trip, which, as Ingram wrote, 'certainly added to his personal comfort but seemed to me to be a bit of an extravaganza.' Four years later he was with George Forrest in Yunnan, where they collected the tender white-flowered *Jasminum polyanthum* and two mahonias. One, *M. lomariifolia*, with particularly long, handsome leaves, grows in the Courtyard at Hidcote. The other, *M. siamensis*, even more tender, flourished in Johnston's garden at Serre de la Madone.

By the late 'twenties, the last phase of garden-making at Hidcote, the most important influence on Johnston seems to have been the quixotic Norah Lindsay who made an extraordinary garden of her own at Sutton Courtenay in Oxfordshire. Like

(*Left*) Norah Lindsay in her garden at Sutton Courtenay in Oxfordshire in 1904

Peto, she had Italy in her bones. 'I would have been a much lesser gardener had I not worshipped at the crumbling shrines of the ancient garden gods of Florence and Rome,' she wrote fruitily, describing her garden in *Country Life* in May 1931. Many influential gardeners of the time asked for her advice. She flitted from Sir Philip Sassoon's theatrical estate at Port Lympne in Kent, to the Astors at Cliveden in Buckinghamshire, to the Marquess of Lothian at Blickling in Norfolk, to the 'too beastly-rich Trittons' at Godmersham in Kent, and, according to her obituary in *The Times*, could 'trace out a whole garden with the tip of her umbrella'. She also stayed with Bobbie James at St Nicholas, which is where she may have met Johnston.

An abundant fecundity was the hallmark of her style: masses of flowers, an eclectic mixture of the rare and the common with a high proportion of self-seeded *arrivistes*. 'Wherever the flowers themselves have planned the garden, I gracefully retire, for they are the guiding intelligences and strike where we fumble.' She used exotic eremurus with cottagey hollyhocks, the 'bloodless candelabra' of Vatican sage (*Salvia turkestanica*) with flaming poppies and sunflowers. She adored roses and had a whole hedge of *Rosa damascena* and another of Penzance roses mixed with sweetbriar. According to her daughter, Nancy, it was Norah who persuaded Johnston to plant the Rose Borders at Hidcote. And, reading Vita Sackville-West's description of the garden in 1949 with its 'spilling abundance' and the dwarf campanula that, 'after the Hidcote principle, had been allowed to seed itself also in brilliant patches wherever it did not rightly belong', it seems likely that her influence permeated the rest of the garden too. You can imagine her egging Johnston on to acquire the ostrich and the flamingoes that once perched precariously in the pool (now a bog garden) at the entrance to Westonbirt, the informal area of trees and shrubs named after the Holford arboretum. Johnston had hoped that Norah Lindsay would come to live at Hidcote when he departed permanently for his house in the South of France, but she died in 1948, the year he left.

One of the herbaceous beds in the Blickling parterre designed by Norah Lindsay

CHAPTER TWO
MAKING THE GARDEN

An archaeologist mapping the development of the garden at Hidcote would recognise several different phases: an initial push (pre-1914) that encompassed little more than the area within the brick walls of the original garden, a second stage (1914–20) that gave birth to the Stilt Garden, the gazebos and Mrs Winthrop's Garden to the west, and a final bold phase (1920–30) that flung the garden south along the Long Walk and into Westonbirt. The lack of documentary evidence makes it difficult to plot exactly how the garden developed, for Lawrence Johnston made no plans, kept no notes or diaries relating to the garden, wrote no articles and makes only the most fleeting appearances in memoirs of the period. Only a few old photographs give us a clue as to what was happening when.

In the seven years between Johnston and his mother coming to Hidcote and the start of the First World War, it is not surprising that development was contained mostly around the house. The approach to a house and the scenes that present themselves immediately from the windows are the chief concern of most new garden owners. There is no evidence that either Johnston or his mother had previous experience in garden-making. With their peripatetic life-style, it seems unlikely that they had ever stayed anywhere long enough to see a tree grow. Certainly, any experienced garden-maker would have thought twice about choosing this particular site for his life's work, despite the superb view over the Vale of Evesham. The land is set high (600 feet) and, until Johnston started planting his evergreen oaks, his tapestry hedges and elegant avenues of beech and holly, was conspicuously exposed. The terrain sloped in a potentially awkward way, the incline generally to the south, with a rise to the west, level only to the north. There was a

(Right) Gertrude Winthrop, Johnston's mother

small stream which came into the garden at its eastern boundary and a cedar tree, planted too close to the house to be ideal.

Johnston, who had fought as a naturalised Briton in the Boer War, was in 1907 still engaged in his army career. During those first seven years in his new home, he would not have been living permanently at Hidcote. Army records show postings during that period in Aldershot and Hythe. It is even possible that, at the beginning, it was Johnston's mother, Gertrude Winthrop, who had the greatest influence upon the garden. It was the money she had inherited from her two husbands, a

The phlox garden (now called the White Garden) around 1910, before the encircling yew hedge had been planted and when the bird topiary was still very new

Baltimore banker and a New York barrister, that had bought the property and she also held the strings of the garden purse. Of the two, she would have had more time to devote to it.

The pre-1914 garden encompassed what is now the Old Garden, the White Garden and the Maple Garden (though not then growing white flowers or maples). It took in the Circle and the Bathing Pool Garden, though the pool, in its first configuration, was a measly thing, surrounded by a fussy fan-shaped arrangement of beds. The house, originally a reasonably compact stone farmhouse, was greatly extended to the west by its new owners, who, at a stroke, doubled its size. The original farmyard to the north of the house was transformed into a tidy entrance courtyard. The farm buildings grouped round three sides of the yard were disguised with climbers and creepers. When it became obvious that Johnston was never going to become a farmer, as he and his mother had first thought, the buildings themselves were converted to other uses. One became a squash court, another a badminton court. The small building to the left of the lower entrance became a private chapel for Johnston who, quite early in adolescence, had converted to Catholicism.

Though it was 1922 before he hired his first professional Head Gardener, a highly skilled man called Frank Adams, there never seems to have been any shortage of labour, drawn from the village of Hidcote Bartrim. There was a permanent staff of five gardeners with more part-time help brought in when it was needed. Apart from his own valet and chauffeur, Johnston had a butler as well as house-keeper and a large domestic staff. Tennis was always a popular pastime at Hidcote, on the hard courts beside the Kitchen Garden, and Johnston played the piano and painted. Never, in the whole of his life, did he have to face the tedium of earning his own living. But never, even after his mother's death in 1926, did he have control of her considerable capital. Construction work in the garden is not well-founded. Effects were created at speed and with whatever materials were to hand. His numerous plant houses and shelters were not the magnificent ornamental conservatories that any manufacturer of the time would have been glad to put up for him. The biggest, by the lily pool, had a back made of twin walls of wooden board, filled with sawdust for insulation.

The essence of Hidcote is, as Graham Stuart Thomas put it, 'a garden of boundless variety soberly controlled'. Firm architectural lines, the lines of the gardens in France and Italy where Johnston had spent so much of his youth, were to contain an eclectic, abundant collection of plants. Living hedges stand in for masonry, topiaried box and yew for sculpture. But given the slightly peculiar lie of the land, architectural lines had occasionally to be smudged. The two big borders of the Old Garden are not of equal size, and the wide grass path that separates them makes a skew line at the entrance from the Circle to accommodate the disparity. The boundary of the White Garden is wider on its north side than on the opposite south. The vista from the Circle through the Fuchsia Garden to the far grass roundel follows the line of the brick wall of the Old Garden, which is not quite at right angles to the main vista through the Red Borders and the Stilt Garden. In order to line up this vista of circles leading south, Johnston had to place the Bathing Pool well off-centre in its enclosure, touching the boundary one side, leaving wide borders on the other. Sleight of hand and abundant planting (as round the wholly uncircular boundary of the Circle) disguise the difficulties he faced.

A few early photographs taken c.1910 show how the garden looked during the first phase of development. The entrance to the garden would not have been, as now, via the garden yard, but directly from the house over the cedar lawn. Then, as now, steps led down through balusters of clipped box to a small enclosure (the present White Garden) filled with phlox. Newly purchased topiary – rather skeletal birds on top of box pillars – sits at the corners of the beds. There is no yew hedge nor arch between this little enclosure and the thatched cottage beyond, only a low post-and-rail fence. There are minimal box hedges round the four beds and the centre is filled with a circle of grass and a sundial. This is exactly like one designed by Sir Ernest George and heavily recommended by Gertrude Jekyll in the influential gardening books that she published during the first years of the century.

In early photographs of the Maple Garden there is not a maple in sight. It was an area chiefly devoted to peonies, some of which are being put back. But the shape of the enclosure is entirely familiar, with the two oblong central beds in place, edged with minuscule box. The brick retaining walls are there too, together with the purely practical block of steps that brings you up out of the garden by the small stream, which later disappears from view. Wooden

The Maple Garden c.1910, when it was mainly devoted to peonies

tubs stand around on the paving, and the shrubs in the raised side beds have a distinctly well-spaced, newly planted look. More instant topiary (birds again) stood either side of the steps from the cedar lawn down to the Old Garden, planted mostly in grey and pink. The ornamental iron gate that leads from the Old Garden to the Circle was originally a much narrower entrance. A single gate, decorated with ironwork in a heart-shaped pattern, hung there with tall stone pillars either side. When Johnston developed the vista beyond the Old Garden, the stone pillars with their ball finials were dismantled and re-erected further apart. The walls either side were lowered, to give a longer view through into the Circle and beyond to the Red Borders.

The Fuchsia Garden, like the Maple Garden, was laid out with its present pattern of beds in the first phase of the garden's development. The hedge that divides it from the Bathing Pool Garden is shown in its infancy, but with two splendid topiary pieces flanking the downward steps. Ready-grown topiary was evidently an extravagance that Mrs Winthrop was prepared to condone. The beds are planted up with mixtures of annual flowers, though by the time that Hidcote made a grand appearance in

Country Life in August 1930, they seem to have been treated as rose beds. The garden editor, H. Avray Tipping, talks of a show of 'exquisite roses in exquisite condition, the pink "Gruss an Aachen" exceeding in floriferousness'. This same pale pink rose now flourishes in the main borders of the White Garden.

Johnston's first design for the Bathing Pool Garden was not as successful as the present one, which was superimposed in the second phase of the garden's development, just after the end of the First World War. In the original scheme, the pool was a small sunken affair, immediately below the steps from the Fuchsia Garden. Behind it, the ground sloped upwards to a final enclosure, and was filled with a fanned arrangement of wedge-shaped beds. The yew hedges were not in place, though the trees had been planted. Behind them was a heavy trellis screen in squared sections made from rustic poles. The view in the earliest photograph of this area, around 1910, is still completely open through to a cottage and farm buildings beyond. To the right you can see a field gate leading to pasture that later became part of the Upper Stream Garden. The whole area is raw with newness. Even in a slightly

The view from the cedar lawn across the Old Garden towards the Circle *c.*1910. The ornamental iron gate was later removed and the stone pillars rebuilt further apart to make the most of the complex vista beyond

The Fuchsia and Bathing Pool Gardens c.1910. The layout of the beds in the Fuchsia Garden has changed little, but the sunken pool beyond was subsequently much enlarged

later picture, it is still unfamiliar. The hedge has joined up round the back, but still cannot be more than four feet tall. The trellis makes a screen behind the low hedge but is now smothered with rambling roses. More roses garland the hoop that arches over the top of the semicircular steps. It is all much softer, much fussier than the classical, if bloodless, lines of the present enclosure with its architectural portico of clipped evergreen replacing the garlanded hoop of roses and evergreen walls blotting out all sign of the world beyond the garden.

The refinement of the area beyond the gate of the Old Garden began with the outbreak of the First World War and marked the beginning of the second phase of the garden's development. Given the presumed shortage of manpower, it is staggering that any work at all continued in this period, especially as Johnston himself was away for much of it, but the slight evidence that exists suggests that

this was when the small red-brick gazebos were built at the end of the existing double Red Borders and the vista extended further to the west by the very un-English device of the pleached hornbeam stilts. The fine gate must have been added after the war was over. This second phase of development at Hidcote has a markedly different character from the first. The first areas to be gardened – the Maple Garden, the Fuchsia Garden, the first Bathing Pool Garden, the White Garden – had all been laid out on the parterre principle: geometrical arrangements of box-edged beds filled to overflowing with flowers. This was the Arts and Crafts, Mary de Navarro/ Alfred Parsons influence at work. The effect is Olde Worlde, cottagey, with topiary in 'the country tradition of smug broody hens, bumpy doves and coy peacocks', as Vita Sackville-West put it.

The second phase was cool, classical. Longer lines were drawn. Plantings were more severely architectural in their effect. It was during this time that Johnston completed the restrained landscape of the Theatre Lawn with its beech on a raised dais like an altar. This was a massive undertaking and a complete antithesis to the crowded spaces of the first phase of garden-making. So was the Stilt Garden, which channelled the view out to the far western boundary of the garden, making, from the huge semicircular seat that stood at the far end of the cedar lawn, a vista of astonishing variety. There is a *trompe-l'oeil* aspect to it too, seen from the house end. It seems much shorter than it is, as Tipping noted in his *Country Life* article: 'Its level first section looks its length. But beyond that, the rise of the ground brings everything near to you, so that you wonder why the high end gates look so faint and spidery.'

Mrs Winthrop's Garden, hedged on three sides for shelter, but largely open to the south, was probably added in this period, though it may have been earlier. There is some similarity in the curving lines of the brickwork with the first design for the Bathing Pool Garden. This is a Riviera garden: Chusan palms rustling in the background, low brick pedestals for pots of exotics such as agaves and cordylines. It was always (and is still) planted with blue and yellow plants. Large feather cushions in the same colours were scattered about on the generously wide steps.

When the gazebos were in place, it is logical to suppose that the beginnings of the Long Walk must have been laid out, perhaps just as far as the stream. Similarly, with Mrs Winthrop's Garden opening to the south, also overlooking the stream, a garden-maker's instinct would be to dress the foreground a little with planting, so that it is likely the Upper Stream Garden at least was gardened at this time. Meandering and informal new paths would connect Mrs Winthrop's Garden with the Bathing Pool Garden. Likewise, since the Red Borders were well established, it is likely that the Winter Border, lying opposite the north entrance to Mrs Winthrop's Garden, was also part of the plan at this time.

After 1920, when Johnston had broken his ties with the army, the final pieces of the Hidcote design were put into place. First came the Pillar Garden, a logical extension, since it lay alongside the Stilt Garden and squared off the space left between this and Mrs Winthrop's Garden. The Pillar Garden continued the Mediterranean theme of Mrs Winthrop's Garden, the ranks of tall clipped yews quite oddly arranged, but the sloping ground cleverly manipulated into a series of shallow terraces. Behind the Pillar Garden, the steep fall in the ground from the Stilt Garden was again disguised by two generous terraces in the curious alley known as the Terrace. Here Johnston grew a wide variety of rare alpines, sheltered in winter under a framework of wood and glass. The way that Johnston coaxed and boxed the lie of Hidcote's land into this sequence of south-facing terraces is one of the cleverest aspects of the design. Now that it is done, it is easy to underestimate the amount of control that he exerted on the terrain. We are led so inevitably from one level to the next as we wander through the garden, it seems it must always have been so. But it was not.

He showed the same determination to overcome the difficulties inherent in the type of soil at Hidcote. It was quite strongly alkaline, but Johnston wanted to grow rhododendrons, which were hugely fashionable at the time, many new species being introduced by plant hunters in China and the Himalayas. He therefore imported vast quantities of sawdust from local sawmills and used it to create three areas in the garden suitable for growing rhododendrons. He evidently did the job well, for rhododendrons still flourish. You can see them in the narrow north-facing border under the cottage wall in the Old Garden and in stretches along the Stream Garden.

Some time around 1927, when he was in his mid-fifties, Johnston took the brave step of flinging the Long Walk out to the horizon on the south. Its length was fixed by the contours of the land. For maximum impact, it could not have stopped sooner without losing the dramatic effect of the final gates silhouetted against the sky. The hedges either side are hornbeam, which he had used to such clever effect in the Stilt Garden. This monumental exercise may have been carried out in several stages, for Tipping, in 1930, says of the Long Walk, 'It is bent, the fall of the first half being balanced by the equal rise of the second half.' This is patently not true of the Long Walk in its present form. When he saw it, did it perhaps end at the present boundary of the Lower Stream Garden, when the downward and upward slopes of the walk would indeed have been of roughly equal length? Westonbirt then perhaps occupied only the lower half of the area behind the

Long Walk. But, although it thrust the garden out on to a limb, Johnston's final resolution to push the Long Walk out further was an admirable one. And it gave him the opportunity to enlarge his collection of trees and shrubs in Westonbirt, for collecting was the passion of his last ten years at Hidcote. No attempt was made to modify the terrain here and you can still see the pattern of wide ridge and furrow that characterises the drainage system of old arable farmland.

When Tipping wrote his glowing report for *Country Life* in 1930 (the garden was open that summer at a shilling a head in aid of the Children's London Garden Fund), Hidcote was approaching its peak. The complex structure with its corridors and rooms was finally complete. The magnificent tapestry hedges dividing the rooms had grown to maturity. The collection of plants within them represented the culmination of years of discerning plantsmanship. Tipping talks of *Lilium centifolium* eight feet high in the entrance courtyard and *Plagianthus betulinus* with birch-like foliage and dense panicles of white flowers sheltering under a barn wall. In the Old Garden were more domestic plantings of tulips followed by *Eremurus robustus* and *Sidalcea* 'Sussex Queen'. There were pink snapdragons here, feathery wands of *Tamarix aestivum*,

roses (including the vanished variety 'Prince of Bulgarie'), and sugar pink dahlias.

The chief loss to the present garden is the wide range of plant shelters that existed in Johnston's time. Tipping mentions a 'low but ample shed' in the entrance yard 'converted into a shady camellia house, with space left in it to accommodate a luncheon table'. 'Nearly all our zealous horticulturists have a perhaps exaggerated yearning for half hardies,' he continued, 'Mr Johnston has cleverly developed the idea of winter shelters for warm climate subjects.' In the main garden there were both shady and sunny raised borders with movable glass roofs where borderline cistuses, *Arbutus canariensis*, *Dendromecon rigida*, *Calceolaria violacea* and other tender subjects overwintered in comfort. The biggest of the shelters was in the Kitchen Garden, lying between the lily pool and the boundary through to the Rose Borders. 'It takes the form of a great, moderately heated glasshouse,' wrote Tipping, 'of which the whole front, including the pipes on this side, are removable for the summer season. Thus it becomes not only an area of much botanic interest, but is an attractive resort at all seasons.' When the south side lay open, he said, the whole thing looked more like a pergola than a glasshouse, filled with extraordinary exotics such as *Haemanthus*

Mrs Winthrop's Garden in summer

One of the winter plant shelters in which Johnston raised
tender exotics, photographed in 1930

katherinae, which Johnston had collected on the
slopes of Mount Kilimanjaro and *Gordonia axillaris*,
with large white flowers like a eucryphia, each with
a tassel of yellow stamens.

This extraordinary collection surprisingly sur-
vived the Second World War and the post-war fuel
crises, the gardeners routinely manhandling three
tons of glass each May and October, when the plants
were shrouded for winter. Early in 1954, however,
all the plants and shrubs in this shelter were hit by an
exceptionally bitter spell of weather. In June that
year, the Trust decided, with regret, that the
building, which was badly in need of repair, should
be demolished and the few remaining plants moved
to the glasshouse adjoining the house. Eventually
this too was emptied and became a cafeteria.

After the last great push of the Long Walk,
Hidcote became essentially a summer garden for its
owner, as Johnston spent more and more time at La
Serre de la Madone. Each autumn the same convoy
set out from Gloucestershire – the chauffeur, Fred
Daniels, in the Bentley with the luggage, Johnston
in his Lancia. Frank Adams, the Head Gardener,
resisted Johnston's urgings to accompany him to the
South of France and stayed put in Gloucestershire.
Frensham, a young gardener trained by Johnston's
friend Bobby James at St Nicholas in Yorkshire,
went instead to Menton, while the Adams family
moved into the manor as caretakers. This routine
continued until the outbreak of war, when Johnston, with other expatriate Britons, was evacuated
from France in an overloaded collier and brought
back to England. By the end of the war he had made
up his mind to hand Hidcote over to the National
Trust and return to France.

CHAPTER THREE
LETTING GO

Hidcote, which the National Trust took over in 1948, was the first important garden to come into its care. In the immediate post-war period, the Trust was still largely land-orientated and owned only six country houses. There was no gardens adviser and no system in place for running a garden. An added problem was an acute shortage of funds. Hidcote came to the Trust without an endowment and in the first years, when visitors were few and the need for repairs pressing, this caused huge problems.

Johnston, an only child and unmarried, had no close relatives to whom he wished to leave Hidcote. His plan, after the war, was to retire to his garden at Menton on the French Riviera, where the climate suited his health. But before he could do that, he wanted to be sure that Hidcote was in good hands. At one stage, he considered leaving it to his friend and neighbour, Lord Barrington, at Nether Lypiatt Manor, but Barrington did not want it. It must have been after this unexpected setback that he began to think of the Trust, egged on, it seems, by Lady Colefax, a prominent society hostess of the time.

The first mention of the possible bequest comes in James Lees-Milne's diary for Friday, 5 February 1943. Lees-Milne, the son of a Worcestershire neighbour of Johnston and the Trust's first Historic Buildings Secretary, was invited to a luncheon party by the indefatigable Sibyl Colefax, but in the event she stayed in bed with bronchitis:

Norah Lindsay acted hostess in her place. She was wearing a flat, black hat like a pancake on the side of her head, pulled down over one eye. It was adorned with cherry-coloured buttons. Her white frilled blouse had more cherry buttons. She is kittenish, stupid-clever, and an amusing talker ... On my left was Laurie Johnston, who had just seen my father at Hidcote ... After luncheon, which was delicious, Laurie Johnston took me aside to ask if the National Trust would take over Hidcote garden without

endowment after the war, when he intended to live in the South of France for good. He is a dull little man, and just as I remember him when I was a child. Mother-ridden. Mrs Winthrop, swathed in grey satin from neck to ankle, would never let him out of her sight.

Nothing further happened until the summer, though Lees-Milne must have mentioned this possible new acquisition to his superiors at the Trust. On 6 July that year he visited Hidcote with his father and had tea with Lawrence Johnston:

No reference was made by him to the National Trust. The garden is not only beautiful but remarkable in that it is full of surprises. You are constantly led from one scene to another, into long vistas and little enclosures, which seem infinite. Moreover the total area of this garden does not cover many acres. Surely the twentieth century has produced some remarkable gardens on a small scale. This one is also full of rare plants brought from the most outlandish places in India and Asia. When my father and Laurie Johnston were absorbed in talk I was tremendously impressed by their profound knowledge of a subject which is closed to me.

A year after the end of the war, the question of Hidcote's future had still not been resolved. In September of 1946 James Lees-Milne describes visiting Sibyl Colefax in hospital. She had still not let go of the idea that the Trust was the only proper answer to the question of Hidcote's future, 'talking enthusiastically about Laurie Johnston's garden'. But the question of how the Trust was to keep it up with no funds seemed insuperable.

A letter from Lady Colefax to James Lees-Milne is the first document in the Trust's voluminous Hidcote archive. In an eminently practical note, written in hasty pencil from her London house at 19 Lord North St, in the late spring of 1947, she urges him to clinch the matter of Hidcote sooner rather

Lawrence Johnston in old age with his beloved dachshunds on the Theatre Lawn

than later. She had been visiting the garden with Vivien Leigh. 'Do get him tied up,' she wrote:

You see he is not 'gaga' but has *no* memory. I did say that I believed he would get off Income Tax on Gardens. If J. put down £10,000 that would be enough to finance the transfer? J. has *no* relations. He has been v. seedy with dermatitis but tho' in bed was bright as a button ... Selling the house wd. be easy – the farm is a good one – the kitchen garden superb qua stock and condition (it supplied four or more huge hospitals during the war).

Lees-Milne promptly despatched a note to Johnston, suggesting that they should perhaps meet to talk about the future of Hidcote. Johnston replied in his strong firm handwriting (not a hint of gaga in that), welcoming the idea and confirming that he had decided to make the property over to the National Trust.

In his report of the visit Lees-Milne considered the options available to the Trust. The house, he said, was pleasant, and could probably be let furnished. The farm of about 280 acres was in good hands, the garden 'probably unsurpassed'. The problem remained the cost of upkeep:

Major Johnston considers that five gardeners are the maximum that would be required. He cannot provide any endowment in money and the Trust would only receive revenue from the letting of the house and the farm tenant.

Johnston was unable to help further, because, much to his disgust, his mother had left him only the interest on her considerable estate, which would pass to cousins on his death.

At its meeting in June 1947 the Historic Buildings Committee recommended that the Trust should accept Hidcote, provided that some endowment was forthcoming and that the gardens could be fully maintained. The Committee suggested that a curator or custodian with proper horticultural qualifications should be installed to superintend the gardens. It was a wise proviso.

At a Finance Committee meeting the following day Harold Nicolson, husband of Vita Sackville-West and co-creator of their garden at Sissinghurst, promised to approach the Royal Horticultural Society to see if they would contribute towards the upkeep of the gardens at Hidcote. Lees-Milne wrote a diplomatic letter to Johnston telling him that the Trust had agreed to accept the property if it could, but pointing out the difficulties of taking on Hidcote without any endowment to keep it up in the manner to which it was accustomed.

On behalf of the RHS Lord Aberconway replied promptly that Nicolson's suggestion was not in their line of country. 'We could not provide funds for a garden rather remote from most of our Fellows,' he continued, 'Nor have we the personnel to supervise the garden and keep it as it should be.' Kew, who were next in line in the search for funds, were equally pessimistic.

Sibyl Colefax, who did much to save the Hidcote garden

The view through the Stilt Garden gates at dusk

In August of that year the Chief Agent, Hubert Smith, was despatched to Hidcote to investigate possibilities of adding to the income and reducing the deficit that the National Trust could expect if it took on the property. There were only two ways he could see of doing this. First, to let the manor to a rich and knowledgeable tenant who would pay a substantial proportion of the expenses of the garden. Second, to increase substantially the numbers of visitors to the garden. This he thought highly unlikely. 'It struck me', he said, 'as the type of garden that would mainly appeal to connoisseurs and experts.'

By spring of the following year, 1948, the Trust had decided to try a different way of financing Hidcote – and any future garden properties. It established a Gardens Fund for legacies and donations specifically earmarked for garden properties. It also decided to set up a Gardens Committee to advise on questions of policy. But meanwhile

Johnston was getting edgy. The nearer the time came for him to depart permanently to his house in France (a move dictated by the iniquities, as he saw them, of the British tax system), the more loath he was to give up his garden in England.

By the middle of June Johnston had evidently decided that he wasn't going to let go entirely. In a letter to Aberconway, he writes, 'Of course I should like it if I could come back here for short periods in the summer. There is so much I have planted that I should like to see grown. For that prevalidge [sic] I might be able to contribute to the expences [sic]. I should have to consult my lawyer about that.' The tone of Johnston's letters became steadily more aggrieved as the summer of 1948 wore on. He had made plans to return permanently to France in September, he told the Trust, and if they did not give him rights of residence in his house, he would remove all the furniture and the family portraits.

To Lees-Milne he wrote saying he found the whole affair very unsatisfactory. The Trust, he said, 'allow me nothing in return for their eventual entire possession of Hidcote. Under those circumstances I had better keep it.' With rather more urgency than on his previous visits, Lees-Milne went to soothe the ruffled feathers. 'Walked round the garden with Lawrence Johnston,' he wrote in his diary on 26 June:

He said he was incensed by a letter he had received from the Trust and had now decided no longer to 'give' us Hidcote. After much discussion and persuasion he agreed to leave it by will, if I would witness his codicil. The garden is a dream of beauty. The old-fashioned rose garden smelled as fragrant as I have always imagined a garden in a French Gothic tapestry might smell. Lawrie Johnston was very nice to me.

The strings attached to Johnston's transfer of Hidcote to the National Trust increased with each exchange of letters. In July, writing to Lord Esher, then Chairman of the Trust, Johnston said the transfer was dependent on him being 'left my house here and control of the garden'. He proposed to come back for three months each summer, which the law allowed him to do without making him liable again for English tax. If the Trust didn't agree to these terms, he wouldn't mind if the whole thing fell through, he said bullishly.

Lees-Milne proposed to Johnston that he should bring Lord Esher on a visit. Wheeling in the big guns, he felt, might finally bring this protracted business to a close. Johnston agreed to the visit. 'I expect to go to France about the 1st of September,' he wrote in reply:

I think the present staff in the garden can carry on. I am head gardener but they have been here so long that they automatically do the work pretty well and if you can spare the time to come here occasionally I believe it would pan out allright. Albert Hawkins is the only real gardener. He is a *great plantsman* and cultivator but he has not much head for planning ahead. He also runs a big allotment at his home and I am afraid might give that priority if there was no one looking after him ... The other three are very jealous of Albert but they do their work pretty well but I don't think would stand Albert over them. Of course a young head gardener would be best but greatly increase the expences and be certain to alter the character of the garden which is largely a *wild garden* in a formal setting. I hope to come here for three months in the summer.

'Bring petrol coupons,' commanded Lord Esher before the party set off on the journey to Hidcote. Lawrence Johnston and his lawyer, plus Nancy Lindsay, Norah Lindsay's daughter, were waiting for them. 'Lawrie J. signed the deed of gift like a lamb so, since he leaves for abroad in a fortnight, the place may be said to be saved,' wrote Lees-Milne in his diary on 27 August 1948:

This has been a struggle but it is accomplished ... Miss Lindsay is like an old witch, very predatory and interfering. She maintains that she has been deputed by L.J. to supervise these gardens in his absence abroad. We were not overcome with gratitude. Anyway no mention of this condition was made either by L.J. or his solicitors before the signing. Sibyl Colefax will be delighted that the deed she worked so hard to bring about has been done.

Verbena 'Lawrence Johnston', which can be found in the Red Borders in summer

CHAPTER FOUR
THE TRUST LEARNS TO GARDEN

In the upper echelons of the National Trust there was a general feeling of relief that the long drawn out saga of Hidcote was finally resolved. Only the Trust's lawyer sounded a note of alarm. He had understood, he said, in the pedantic, but exact way of the legal profession, that the acquisition of Hidcote depended on there being adequate funding to maintain it. In his opinion that funding was not in place. He was right.

There was also a new problem: Miss Nancy Lindsay, self-appointed guardian, in Johnston's absence, of the Hidcote soul. Having spent most of her life in her mother's far-reaching shadow, Nancy stayed on after her death in 1948 at the Manor Cottage at Sutton Courtenay, living a rather hand-to-mouth existence, selling plants from a nursery that she had established after plant-hunting trips in Persia. She specialised in old-fashioned roses and was considered perhaps a better plantswoman than her mother, but not as good a gardener.

Lees-Milne was sufficiently unsettled by her presence at the official transfer of Hidcote to the Trust to write immediately to Lord Aberconway, the chairman of the Trust's new Gardens Committee. 'Of course, she knows the Hidcote garden like the back of her hand,' he wrote, 'but she is very proprietary and I do not know how well she gets on with the gardeners there.' Aberconway replied robustly from his garden at Bodnant in north Wales that they would have to deal with that difficulty as it arose. At its meeting on 14 September the Gardens Committee instructed the Chief Agent that, in accordance with Major Johnston's wishes, Miss Lindsay was to supervise the garden during Johnston's absence abroad.

In her small determined hand, with much underlining, on pages torn from an exercise book, Nancy

Lindsay compiled a nine-page letter to Lord Esher, relating, in rather too much detail, her views on the garden at Hidcote. Among the clipped, dry memos of the archives, her garrulous screeds stand out like birds of paradise caught up in the company of ravens:

My position is that of a very old and devoted friend of Johnny's who knows Hidcote as well as he does himself . . . I know his plans for every yard of it. And all last summer he has walked and talked with me about what was to be seen to, saying 'You must be me, Nancy, and see the gardeners don't forget anything or make any mistakes.' He was very much against the idea of installing a grand head gardener, who would 'tidy-up' the lush and rather jungly effect Johnny likes.

I am not being paid for this. I am too fond of Johnny to accept a 'salary' from him, but he insists on paying my expenses. My accounts for any expenses incurred go in to Mr Snelling [Johnston's lawyer]. I refused a practically blank cheque from Johnny which with delightful generosity he tried to make me accept . . . I am to 'help myself' as a return for all I do for Johnny.

The problem of the Kitchen Garden was aired at length. The gardeners, said Miss Lindsay, wasted too much time growing vegetables which they sold at a profit to themselves. This 'has been a very sore point with Johnny'. She hoped the National Trust would understand this problem and make sure that the vegetable garden did not flourish at the expense of the flowers. A final breathless paragraph assured the Trust that she only wanted to do what was best for Hidcote.

The Lindsay pamphlet, as it became known, did not go down well. 'I pass this sinister and long winded letter to you for action,' wrote Lord Esher to James Lees-Milne. 'The Gardens Committee must try and get rid of her.' But she blithely continued to send more letters, concurring with the Trust's decision to promote Albert Hawkins, one of the team of four at Hidcote, to Head Gardener. 'Though Albert can always refer to me of course ... I shall be over at Hidcote about once a month anyway of course as "supervisor" and continue giving Hidcote all the plants from my own garden which I can manage to ...' She was just off, she said, to stay with Johnston in France for three weeks.

The question of the Kitchen Garden continued to rumble. In November 1948 Captain Inns, Johnston's land agent from Truslove & Harris in Stratford, who had been retained to keep an eye on the Hidcote estate, wrote to the Trust saying that Miss Lindsay had stopped all sale of produce from the Kitchen Garden. This, he said, seemed a pity. The revenue to the estate was small, but it was better than nothing. 'We seem to be heading for a prize row,' said the Chief Agent cheerfully, promising that he would try to discover exactly what was happening to the surplus plants at Hidcote.

A year later a new idea emerged for the Kitchen Garden. Perhaps it could be used to raise shrubs and plants propagated from material in the garden? By then, too, the Trust's Gardens Committee had begun to realise the difficulties of running a garden by remote control. Plants did not stay in their place like furniture. They decided they needed a local committee, responsible for seeing that the garden continued along the right track. A committee might also usefully dissipate the influence of the over-proprietorial Miss Lindsay, though of course she would have to be invited to be a member.

Jack Rathbone, then Secretary of the Trust, approached Major Kenneth Shennan (a gardener of 'faultless taste', he had been assured) at Shipton Oliffe Manor, close to Hidcote, to see if he would take on the position of chairman of this committee. 'What this place really needs is a boss who is not only a great and knowledgeable gardener but also

Heather Muir, an important member of the Hidcote garden committee, in her own garden at nearby Kiftsgate

a man of taste,' he wrote in October 1949. Who could refuse such an invitation? Shennan accepted graciously:

I owe a great deal to Hidcote and to Major Johnston in days gone by and I count it an honour to be asked to join in running this garden which stands for a type of culture which, alas, is likely to be lost from now onwards in the life of England.

Heather Muir, Johnston's neighbour at Kiftsgate, also accepted the invitation to join the local committee, though she hinted that there would be a good many difficulties to face. So did Nancy Lindsay, as Johnston's 'seeing eye'. Shennan was uneasy:

I do not wish to find myself as chairman being told at any moment that Miss Lindsay's 'seeing eye' has detected a course of action which will be upsetting to Major Johnston. If she has this special and privileged qualification to put at the disposal of Hidcote Gardens, she either ought to be chairman of the committee or not on it at all.

Shennan's concerns were well founded, but Rathbone persuaded him to suppress them and the local committee had its first meeting on Friday, 17 February 1950 with the Cambridge don Joseph de Navarro, another friend and neighbour (he was now the owner of his mother, Mary Anderson's Court Farm, Broadway) as the fourth member.

Eighteen months after the handover, in the spring of 1950, Jack Rathbone visited Hidcote during a tour of the Trust's Midland properties. 'I got a definite impression that these gardens had gone downhill,' he said. 'The grass was unmown, hedges unkempt and the place looked slightly forlorn. I think Hawkins badly wants more bossing.' The Chief Agent was not surprised. In his opinion the Hidcote problem would only be resolved by their finding a keen gardening tenant to take control. Rathbone returned a month later to find the grass still unmown, the camellia shelter badly in need of repair and the frames crying out for paint.

The local committee, meeting only once every three months, did not prove to be the instant saviour of the garden that the National Trust had hoped, although it set in train, as best it could, the rejuvenation and replanting of various parts of the garden. An extra complication arose when Johnston returned to Hidcote for the summer of 1950. He did not take kindly to the fact that the garden was open to the public, albeit only three afternoons a week. 'I do not think it need be more than once a week,' he wrote grandly to Rathbone:

Even that means that no work is done and labour [which he was no longer paying for] is a very great expense. I could as a matter of fact not open it at all when I am here and I am very much tempted to do that . . . To me it spoils the pleasure of a garden which should be a place of repose and to get away from this world.

Johnston, now, sadly, beginning to exhibit all the signs of senile dementia that had affected his mother towards the end of her life, was not mollified by the Trust's tactful reply. Even the gardeners, whom he had always supported, came under attack. 'Albert Hawkins seems to be entirely occupied growing fancy geraniums in the greenhouse,' wrote Johnston to Rathbone that same summer:

They are very lovely but are chiefly indoor plants and don't contribute to the beauty of the garden. I shall want some of them for the south of France. I think you could without harm let him go . . . He must not take *the greenhouse plants with him.* Could you send someone to give him notice and to take charge? . . . If I am to live here I must be master in my own garden which I distinctly am not now though *I made the whole of it.*

Hawkins, who knew Johnston better than anybody, told the Trust not to worry:

If you get letters from him don't take much notice of them but if you don't understand what he is writing about, don't be afraid to let me know . . . I am afraid he is going like his mother went, very sad. We have been to a few nurseries and ordered plants for Hidcote, if there is any trouble from Major Johnston please let me know as I can put things right.

Things did not seem at all right to Johnston, however, as he wrote again to Rathbone. He wanted to take some more of the Hidcote plants back to his garden in the South of France:

It seems absurd to me that I have to ask you for my own plants and I should very much like to have the garden in my own hands again. Is it possible for me to

do so? I should like to have your opinion and I will also consult my lawyers.

Rathbone replied with a letter of brilliant diplomacy:

Although these gardens are now the property of the Trust and in your absence controlled by us, we do of course welcome your return and when you are at Hidcote your advice on the management of the gardens will be respected by the Trust. Of course there is no objection to your taking plants from Hidcote for your garden in France.

A list of these plants, prepared at the time, is a useful indicator of what was growing in the garden in Johnston's time, but the Trust, although it made an inventory of any house that came into its possession, never made an inventory of this, its first garden. There were two fuchsias on the list, 'The Doctor', a single variety with salmon pink tube and sepals, the corolla a deep reddish orange, and another listed as 'Duke of York', which no longer seems to exist. There were two sorts of day lily, one lemon, one golden. Johnston wanted several roses, including *Rosa gallica versicolor* and the cluster-flowered rose 'Nathalie Nypels' bred in 1919, which continues to give a remarkable display in the borders of the Old Garden. Hoheria was on the list, as were ten camellias and the fine Michaelmas daisy *Aster × frikartii*, also still flowering in the Old Garden.

With his plants, Johnston departed for his French garden in September, leaving one more bomb behind him. This time, Nancy Lindsay, his 'seeing eye', was the victim. 'Hawkins tells me that you left instructions with him that Miss Lindsay was to have nothing to do with the gardens or stay in the house,' wrote the Trust's agent to Johnston in France. Miss Lindsay, evidently unaware of this veto, was intending to come and stay at Hidcote in two weeks time. What should he do? Johnston replied in a curt note, 'I have certainly not asked Miss Lindsay to stay in my house and I much prefer that she should not have anything to do with my property.' After that, of course, it was only a short time before Nancy

(Opposite) Hydrangea aspera macrophylla, Physostegia virginiana 'Alba' and pink phlox in the Pillar Garden (summer)

The pool in the Pine Garden, with a potted agave and floods of agapanthus in the foreground (August)

Lindsay was eased off the local garden committee. 'She belongs to the past history of Hidcote which we must escape if we are ever to get control of the future,' said Shennan percipiently. Miss Lindsay, stout trooper that she was, took the news on the chin. 'I've never thanked you for your charming letter!!!!!' she wrote to Rathbone, as though she had received a wonderful invitation rather than a kick in the teeth. She hoped to keep in touch with them all, she said, and sent Rathbone a copy of her rose list:

My mother of course was the first disciple of Miss Willmott's to collect these 'old' roses again and she originally started Major Johnston off and gave him nearly all his first plants. In fact she practically made that old rose garden for him originally; the only part of lovely Hidcote that was an 'afterthought', planned by a person other than Johnny himself.

That was not quite the end of the story, however. When Johnston died in 1958, Nancy Lindsay inherited his house at Serre de la Madone and the contents of his Monte Carlo bank account. She immediately put the place up for sale, but asked the Cambridge University Botanic Garden to collect whatever plants, seeds or cuttings they wanted from the garden there. These, she hoped, would provide a living memorial to Johnston and his work.

Nancy Lindsay's departure did not solve the problem of managing the garden at Hidcote. Gardening by committee was an inherently impossible proposition, however well meant, and the balance sheets, produced at the end of each year, continued to alarm those at head office in charge of the Trust's finances. The Trust had originally counted on being able to let the house to a gardening tenant, who would provide finance and direction for the garden. There was rather a vague gentleman's agreement that Johnston would also make some contribution to its running expenses.

By the time of the takeover there had been a subtle shift, entirely in Lawrence Johnston's favour. Johnston wished to retain the right to use the house in the summer. This precluded any idea of a tenant. In the final note prepared by the Chief Agent, the Trust found itself liable for 'all the outgoings and expenses in connection with the property including the wages of Mrs Hughes who will look after the inside of the house and the insurance of Major Johnston's furniture and the feeding of his dogs.' There were four gardeners: Ted Pearce (68), who started when Johnston first came to Hidcote in 1907, Walter Bennet (50), who had been at the garden for 30 years, as had Albert Hawkins (55), whom the Trust later made Head Gardener. Sid Nichols (47), Bennet's brother-in-law, made the fourth. Three of the gardeners received £4 10s a week. Ted Pearce, whom Johnston looked on as senior gardener, received £5. The outgoings were clear enough, the incomings less plain.

Meanwhile, work was set in hand for the first official opening in the spring of 1949. A new mower was urgently needed but, in the pinched years after the Second World War, even this was a major obstacle. The old established firm, Ransome's, wrote to say they were sorry but they were still dealing with orders from 1946. Signposts were set up to guide visitors through the complicated network of lanes that led to Hidcote. A board was prepared for Hidcote's front gate: 'Open 1 April – 31 Oct Wed, Thurs and Sat (2–5) at a fee of 1/-'.

By the time of the opening, the Trust had spent £858 on the property and received, from Johnston, £34. At the end of that first season income from visitors was £58, which at a shilling a head, means that 1,160 people had been to see the garden. More (£90) was made by selling produce but the fuel for the greenhouses alone cost the Trust £100. By 6 July that first year, the deficit at Hidcote stood at £1,650 and 'the prospect of meeting it not bright', reported Rathbone after a meeting with Johnston's lawyers. Only the Gardens Fund, standing at the close of the first season at £6,293, saved the day.

For Albert Hawkins, Head Gardener, however, the year started well, for the Trust had agreed that he could take a display of his beloved geraniums to the Chelsea Flower Show. After closing down during the war years, the show had reopened in 1947 and Lees-Milne was there. He 'made for the Aberconways' tent', as he wrote in his diary, 'and had a scrumptious tea and iced coffee. Then … looked at some of the show. I never knew flowers could be forced into such size: delphiniums 12ft high, begonias like dishes … David Bowes-Lyon dragged me off to see the Hidcote stall of common geraniums which we thought *quelconque*.' But the display got a Banksian medal from the Royal Horticultural Society and Hawkins returned triumphant.

At Sissinghurst, meanwhile, Vita Sackville-West was preparing an article on Hidcote to be printed in the Royal Horticultural Society's journal. She wanted a plan to go with her piece but none could be found. An approach was made to Garrett, Johnston's solicitor. Perhaps there might be one amongst Johnston's papers, enquired the Trust hopefully? There was not. 'As a matter of opinion,' wrote Garrett carefully, 'I should say that Major Johnston never prepared such a plan and did not approach his garden making on quite that sort of basis.' But Vita Sackville-West's sumptuous tapestry of words more than made up for the absence of a map and her article was later reprinted as the first guide to the Hidcote garden.

The Long Walk (May)

Sales of plants continued to bring in some revenue for the Trust. The author Compton Mackenzie wanted seed of a sweet william, cherry red with a white centre. Vita Sackville-West herself asked Rathbone if she could buy a *Hydrangea integerrima* (now known as *H. serratifolia*), the 'creamy, fluffy apparition' she had described in her article on the garden. Hawkins replied that, even for her, there was none. He was in disgruntled mood. The Trust had decided that the trees and shrubs in Westonbirt were in urgent need of thinning. The offending growth was marked and two extra hands hired to help with the work. 'We have not made a start in the arboretum yet,' he wrote to Rathbone in November 1950:

There are so many other jobs that comes first. This will do when it's rough weather and too wet to do digging. At this time of the year we have a lot of shelters to put up, roughly three ton of glass, also a lot of tender plants to get under cover. You mention some of it is overcrowded well this is how Major Johnston like it. I don't know what he will say that's if we cut down all that is marked. I shall not take the blame.

The sympathy of any practical gardener will be with Hawkins in this debate, but for the Trust it was a battle of wills. At the end of November Rathbone complained that the roses had not been pruned, the muck had not been carted, the azaleas not shifted from the Red Borders, the shrubs in Westonbirt still a hopeless tangle. The local committee fared no better. At the end of December Mrs Muir noted that no replanting had been done in the Red Borders and that the leafmould destined for this same border had all been used in the Kitchen Garden. A stern edict went out: 'No leafmould will be put on the kitchen garden unless instructions to that effect are given by the committee.' Hawkins sacked one of the men engaged for the thinning of Westonbirt. And there, at a score of thirty-all, the tournament for the moment was suspended, to be resumed the following spring. At the March meeting of the local committee one of the members demonstrated to the assembled gardeners the correct way to prune roses. The agent reported that Hawkins was 'very worried and upset'. Rathbone sought the advice of Harold Nicolson, who, in his most soothingly patrician

Harold Nicolson and Vita Sackville-West in their garden at Sissinghurst. Both were great admirers of Hidcote

mode, replied, 'Of course even the best head gardeners have their hobbies and unless supervised are inclined to neglect the real work for their own happy pursuits. The head gardener at Hidcote happens to love geraniums, with the result that the propagation of the rarer plants has certainly suffered a decline.' On the other hand, he believed that any visitor to Hidcote would still get 'all the pleasure and instruction which he got in Laurie Johnston's day.'

The year 1950 started well for the Trust with a cheque for £500 brought back from the South of France by Johnston's lawyer. Revenue from visitors increased steadily each year too. By the end of the 1950 season £255 8s 6d had been raised from admission fees. The admission charge had been increased by a massive 50% to 1/6, but more than 3,500 people came to enjoy Hidcote's Red Borders and Stream Garden and long, pleached alleys. Sales of produce realised £121 12s 11d, but even with these vastly improved figures there was still, at the end of the year, a deficit of nearly £1,248 to be made up from the accommodating Gardens Fund. By the end of the next season visitor figures had doubled again with more than 7,000 making the journey to Hidcote, most of them in June, but the deficit remained stubbornly the same.

Lists of plants for sale at Hidcote continue to give a good picture of what was growing in the garden at the time: buddlejas, ceanothus, the double orange day lily, lavender, comfrey (always plenty of *that*), viburnum and several old roses including 'Hebe's Lip', 'Kazanlik' and the invaluable 'Nathalie Nypels'. The notes taken by Shennan's local garden committee provide the only record of the Trust's early education in the matter of running garden properties. There are mentions of the Yellow Garden (probably the garden now known as Mrs Winthrop's), of the need to thin out the Michaelmas Daisy Walk (a feature that no longer exists), to repair the orangery. This was a large structure, clearly shown in old photographs of the garden which was built as a glass lean-to shelter for exotic plants. It opened out on to the lily pond where the clipped Portugal laurels and pots of agaves now stand. In summer the front wall of glass was dismantled to make an open shelter for tender echiums, ginger plants, lush *Fuchsia fulgens*, billardiera, crinums, grevillea, clivia, bomarea and the sweet-smelling *Rhododendron* 'Fragrantissimum'.

There were also eleven large ornamental pots and vases in the shelter, but the garden committee felt that the expense of repairing it could not be justified. They suggested keeping just three of the decorative pots for what was then called the Italian Garden, next to the Bathing Pool Garden, and selling off the rest. A completely new mixed shrub border eventually replaced the shelter and its exotic inhabitants. It remains one of the garden's greatest losses, but with Hidcote still running at a steady loss of around £1,400 a year, it was a decision forced upon the Trust.

The numbers of fingers in the Hidcote pie increased steadily. Lord Aberconway of Bodnant advocated the removal of the apple trees growing along the stream border. Clarence Elliott, the famous nurseryman, was asked to recommend gentians to plant by the fish pond. An order was duly placed for 150 G. *sino-ornata* and 75 G. *hexa-farreri*, but these have long since disappeared. One name, however, was to have a lasting influence on Hidcote, and indeed on all the gardens that came into the Trust's ownership thereafter. This was Graham Stuart Thomas, then a nurseryman and expert rosarian. It was he who made the first approach – writing to Mrs Muir of Kiftsgate, a crucial member of the local garden committee, and offering to label the old roses in the Rose Borders correctly. By the summer of 1953 this had been done.

Thomas was then 44 and, as he made clear to Mrs Muir, was thinking about a change of career: 'At times I find coping with the nursery a bore and want to garden and write in the future, but writing alone is too precarious a living I fear.' Heather Muir felt he might be just the person to install at Hidcote as Curator, his chosen title. Rathbone was less sure, but the advisability of the Trust having some person with special responsibility for gardens among its staff was not lost on him. Two years after his foray among the roses, and seven years after the garden had passed to the Trust, Graham Stuart Thomas secured the appointment as the Trust's Gardens Adviser. The Hidcote course, and the course of all the Trust's gardens thereafter, was set.

CHAPTER FIVE
TOUR OF THE GARDEN

There is no set route round Hidcote, which new visitors occasionally find disconcerting. Think of it instead as intriguing. There are secrets to be discovered here, which no garden, parading itself openly on a plain, can ever offer. There is actually an innate logic in the way that Hidcote is laid out, with two great corridors stretching out at right angles to each other. One runs roughly west from the old cedar tree by the house, through the Old Garden, the Circle, the Red Borders, and the Stilt Hedge to finish in the great view through wrought-iron gates over the Vale of Evesham. The second runs roughly south from the summer-houses through long straight hedges of hornbeam to the gate set on the horizon of the garden, which looks as though it might be the end of the world. Rooms, as in a house, open off the corridors, but these are formed from walls of yew and box, copper beech and hornbeam. You are offered more exits and entrances than you are in a house, and the whole is open to shifting patterns of light and shade and the different moods wrought by seasonal patterns of growth and decay.

In visiting a garden as intricate as Hidcote, the long view is as important as the short. Plants are only one element in a good garden and good groupings of plants only one of the delights that Hidcote has to offer. It is only when you lift your head up from what is on the ground and take note of the wider context of the garden that all its elaborate pieces start to come together. Walk to the end of the lime tunnel and glimpse the view over the stream to the land of Westonbirt beyond. Stand on the curved flight of steps just below Mrs Winthrop's Garden and see how cleverly the garden invites you over the Long Walk, through the tall hedge and gives you just a whisper of what is happening in the Pillar Garden beyond. Most modern gardeners understand plants better than design, but even the most beautiful plant shines brighter in the right setting.

There is also an increasing demand on the part of

Bird topiary and 'White Triumphator' tulips in the White Garden (May)

garden visitors for colour in all parts of a garden and at all seasons. This is not a preoccupation that Johnston shared. Plants had to offer more than colour to find a place in his affections. Overall form, and habit of growth, the shape and texture of a plant's leaves, its scent and – it must be said – its rarity, were all important considerations. And he would not have expected all parts of the garden to be singing equally loudly through spring, summer and autumn. It was a luxury available to those who gardened on this scale (Hidcote covers 10 acres including the Kitchen Garden) that certain areas could be devoted to mass displays that peaked at different times of the year. The Fuchsia Garden at Hidcote is an example of this sort of spectacle. Only the most contrary of visitors will expect a fuchsia garden to be at its best in May.

In planting for the future, the National Trust does not restrict itself only to the varieties in the garden in Johnston's day, partly because there are such scanty records of what he actually planted. Rather, it seeks to develop Hidcote within the architectural framework he established, trying out new plants and new ideas that seem in sympathy with his aims.

The tour following is arranged in three separate sections. The spring tour covers the months of April and May, the summer tour concentrates on the special effects of June, July and August, and the autumn tour encompasses the months of September and October. The numbers against each area correspond with the numbers on the map on the inside back cover.

Spring

1 THE COURTYARD

The space is enclosed by the house and the range of handsome barns. In the corner by the ticket entrance is a handsome large-leaved *Magnolia delavayi*, a slightly tender species from Yunnan. It grows with an equally good foliage plant, *Mahonia lomariifolia*, underplanted with pale pink bergenias. New shoots of peonies will be already showing in the bed against the boundary wall, where a large bush of osmanthus shelters the handsome spiky grey foliage of a red hot poker, *Kniphofia caulescens*. *Ceanothus arboreus* 'Trewithen Blue' spreads itself over the wall of the small chapel with a blue *Clematis alpina* scrambling through the schizophragma next to it. On the south wall *Viburnum × burkwoodii* is in full blossom by mid-April, but you will have to wait until May for the full glory of the wistaria trained over the shop entrance and on the boundary wall. By late May too the fine old rose 'Gloire de Dijon' will already be flowering against the wall of the house. In the border between the two gates there is also a good display from the early rose 'Cantabrigiensis' with masses of pale creamy flowers on graceful stems.

2 THE GARDEN YARD

The tree that dominates the yard, growing against the building in the centre, is a magnificent handkerchief tree, *Davidia involucrata vilmoriniana*. The huge creamy white bracts that give it its common name flutter between the pale green leaves in May. The holly-hedged enclosure with its clipped topiary domes was formerly the drying green and has since been used for selling plants. A superb old wistaria lolls over the corrugated-iron roof of the garden stores beyond. At the beginning of May the flowers are still in fish like bud. The flowers come later in the month. Against the wall of the shop is an unusual false acacia, *Robinia × holdtii*. The blue paint that now is such a feature of Hidcote was the Trust's choice, not Johnston's. 'I should like the entrance gates repainted Snowshill blue instead of the present dowdy yellow-green', wrote the Trust's secretary, Jack Rathbone, shortly after it had taken over the garden. The colour was later adopted throughout. A cousin of the popular annual sweet pea is used as ground cover under the philadelphus. This pea, *Lathyrus vernus*, is perennial, making useful mounds of foliage studded with small, purple flowers.

3 THE THEATRE LAWN

This and the Long Walk are the two lungs in the Hidcote garden, the two spaces where the human form is reduced to a completely different scale. The fine old beach tree on the dais at the end of the lawn (illustrated on p.46) has had to be felled because it had become unsafe; a young beach has been planted in its place. The four hornbeams at the restaurant end were planted to replace earlier beaches. A beautifully clipped yew hedge surrounds the lawn, making a semi-circular apse at the end. Tall ilex oaks, planted by Johnston to remind him of the olive trees of the Mediterranean sling a further screen round the lawn. On the right-hand side, a narrow opening leads through to a wrought-iron screen, a gate and a long beech avenue.

4 THE OLD GARDEN

You can slip into the Old Garden either by the narrow blue-painted door, swagged with pink-flowered *Clematis* × *vedrariensis*, or make a more formal entrance from the Circle. Blue and white, pink and mauve dominate here. The space, bounded by old brick walls, is divided into five long mixed borders, the two centre ones divided by a grass path ten feet wide. The side border under the house wall has mixed narcissus, blue pansies and more *Lathyrus vernus*. Later, towards the end of May, brilliant blue anchusa and white oriental poppies fill the border, and the blue and white theme is kept going the whole of the summer with a changing cast of flowers. Spreadeagled against the brick wall behind this border is the early flowering 'Lawrence Johnston' rose, raised in France in 1923. The semi-double flowers are a rich peach yellow with a pink flush on the outside of the buds.

White, pink and yellow tulips fill the two centre borders, with mounds of pink weigela and blue ceanothus behind. The variegated cornus is more important for foliage than flowers, though in May these will be starting to show. When the tulips are gone, the vivid magenta geranium, *G. psilostemon*, covers the gaps, contrasting well with thalictrum and the pale mauve, almost grey floribunda rose 'Lavender Pinocchio' growing in a corner by the grass path. There are peonies of course – one of Johnston's favourite plants – including the brilliant pink single variety 'China Rose'. Hidcote holds the national collection of these plants. In the shady beds under the cedar, grape hyacinths and scillas jostle

Erythronium 'White Beauty' and *Helleborus orientalis* in the south border of the Old Garden (April)

with blue *Anemone blanda* and the small purple-leaved violet.

In the narrow border under the cottage on the far side of the Old Garden where Johnston imported special soil to grow acid-loving shrubs, erythroniums, cyclamen and *Bergenia ciliata* grow in the shade of the wall. Hellebores and blue *Anemone blanda* make a carpet under the big *Magnolia sinensis*. There are brilliant blue meconopsis and a collection of smaller rhododendrons, including 'Blue Tit' and *R. augustinii*.

5 THE WHITE GARDEN

This symmetrical little enclosure with its matching pairs of coy, stylised topiary birds is a pleasure to be in at any time of the year. The structure is satisfying and the texture of the box which edges the four corner beds contrasts well with the warm, worn tones of the stone paving. The pale-leaved dead nettle 'White Nancy' and white violas scramble around under tulips 'White Triumphator' and artemisia. Acanthus and cabbagey *Crambe cordifolia* make strong mounds of foliage.

6 THE MAPLE GARDEN

By the beginning of May the maples (*Acer palmatum dissectum*) that give the garden its name make soft, feathered mounds of bronze, contrasting well with the shiny, chunky foliage of *Choisya ternata* nearby. The two long thin centre beds are filled with fat hyacinths and in the raised beds either side you will find *Magnolia stellata* and pale mauve and white rhododendrons, which take over as the magnolia is finishing. Stepping stones set in a gravel path lead you past a sunken stream with lush clumps of skunk cabbage and wands of Solomon's seal. On your right as you leave the Maple Garden is a fine tall *Staphylea holocarpa rosea* which was introduced to this country from China the year after Johnston came to Hidcote. The clusters of small pink flowers appear before the leaves are fully grown.

7 THE CIRCLE

The cool grass roundel is surrounded by beds of Rouen lilac (*Syringa × chinensis*), in full flower by the beginning of May. Hellebores and the invalu-

able perennial pea (*Lathyrus vernus*) cover the ground underneath with a random sprinkling of yellow and orange Welsh poppies.

8 THE RED BORDERS

These are at their height in summer when tender exotics such as cordyline and canna emerge from their winter hibernation under glass, but there is much to enjoy in spring too. In April there is the blossom of different cherries in the left-hand border, *Prunus spinosa* 'Purpurea' with *P.* × *cistena* and *P. cerasifera* 'Pissardii'. Pools of purple sage contrast with the extraordinary orange bells of *Fritillaria imperialis*, each spike topped with a pineapple tuft of leaves. Red-flowered pulmonaria carpets the ground where later roses will bloom and the huge rhubarb leaves of *Rheum palmatum* 'Atrosanguineum' glisten in sun or rain. By May mass plantings of tulips dominate the borders, crimson and deep purple. The darkest is 'Queen of Night', springing from mounds of heuchera and backed by the filigree leaves of bronze fennel. Bulk in the borders comes from the purple foliage of the cherries, a purple

Lily-flowered
'Red Shine' tulips and
Rheum palmatum
'Atrosanguineum' in
the south Red Border
(May)

filbert (*Corylus maxima* 'Purpurea') and a Norway maple (*Acer platanoides* 'Crimson King'), but by the end of May the tall-flowering spikes of the rheum and some staggering oriental poppies 'Beauty of Livermere' steal the show. The poppies are particularly good with the spiky foliage of bronze cordylines, which are introduced into the Red Borders as the weather warms up. They are plunged in the ground in their pots. If they are planted out, the root systems develop so extensively they cannot be dug up and repotted in winter. But plunging brings its own problems. The cordylines dry out more quickly than plants with a free root run and need special care with watering.

9 THE STILT GARDEN

Helleborus corsicus flourishes in the small beds round the pavilions, contrasting with the sword-like foliage of sky blue irises and *Hosta sieboldiana elegans*. Spires of the yellow crown imperial 'Lutea Maxima' dominate the end beds with the foliage of pampas and giant grasses such as *Stipa gigantea* and *Miscanthus sinensis*. By the end of May the stiffly formal blocks of the hornbeam stilts will be bright with new foliage.

10 THE PILLAR GARDEN

This is not to be missed in mid-May, when the peonies are at their best. You can see the bronze shoots already pushing through the ground in April, providing a backdrop for grape hyacinths and narcissus. Huge blowsy tree peonies 'Souvenir de Maxime Cornu' grow on the top level of the Pillar Garden. In the middle section, between the rows of pillars, you will find *Paeonia arietina* with single pink flowers, together with a paler version of the same species 'Mother of Pearl' and 'Avant Garde'. The borders of pink double peonies 'Mutabilis Plena', running down towards the stream, are slightly later than the singles and are a stunning spectacle in late May. Thick purple ribbons of giant alliums (*A. giganteum*) are massed behind them, fuzzy spheres of purple balanced on four-foot stems. The tall thin spires of 'Amanogawa' cherries that were previously used at the back of these borders have

been replaced with columnar hawthorns (*Crataegus oxyacantha* 'Erectus'), underplanted with mounds of the geranium 'Johnson's Blue' and blue aquilegias. A beautiful large specimen of *Magnolia denudata*, flowering in early spring, spreads its branches over a carpet of herbaceous geraniums and orange poppies.

11 THE TERRACE

These raised beds were once protected by big glass covers, which were removed in summer. This allowed Johnston to grow rare alpines that needed a drier winter than was usually to be had in Gloucestershire. You can still see the footings of the frames that held the glass along the base of the lower retaining wall. The terrace is arranged on two levels with pale creamy potentillas, pinks and mats of sun roses including the sulphur yellow *Helianthemum* 'Jubilee' spilling over the edges of the beds. The pineapple broom *Cytisus battandieri* acts as a backstop before the steps to the pavilion.

12 THE WINTER BORDER

A tall cube of evergreen ilex, Johnston's substitute for the olives of the South of France, nudges against the pavilion. This and the mounds of low-growing *Mahonia japonica* provide a year-round foliage background for the more transient tenants of this border. The handsome tree that dominates it is a pink-flowered *Magnolia campbellii*, slow to come into flower but, when it is established, one of the finest of all the big magnolias. The white flowers of *Viburnum opulus* 'Compactum' will be followed in autumn by translucent bunches of berries. The pale pink *Rhododendron yunnanense*, like all rhododendrons, needs lime-free soil, which Johnston went to great lengths to provide in particular borders.

13 THE LONG WALK

The bold vista is Hidcote's antidote to the tightly packed busyness of the garden rooms grouped either side of it. The dip down to the stream and the hill the other side give the Long Walk a drama it would otherwise lack. You are pulled on towards the tall brick pillars and their acorn-shaped urns to

Alliums and peonies in the Pillar Garden (May)

see what lies on the other side. The view is intensely rural: ploughland, coppice, pasture. When one turns back to look inward, the brick pavilions with their neatly swept-up roofs fill the foreshortened vista.

14 MRS WINTHROP'S GARDEN

Dark blue and yellow is the theme in this garden, with golden creeping Jenny (*Lysimachia nummularia* 'Aurea') in the low beds and golden hop (*Humulus lupulus aureus*) climbing through tripods in the corners. More yellow comes from leopard's bane (*Doronicum* 'Miss Mason') and, later in May, big clumps of day lilies (*Hemerocallis flava*). Blue spreads from violas growing amongst the creeping Jenny and from handsome clumps of anchusa and variegated comfrey. The leaves of the battered Chusan palms (another Mediterranean touch) rustle like brittle ghosts. The boundaries are borrowed from other features: the lime from the lime tunnel; the beech from the long hedge that runs parallel with the Terrace; and the Winter Border and the hornbeam from the Long Walk.

15 THE FUCHSIA GARDEN

Blue scillas grow thickly in the beds where the fuchsias will flourish in the summer. Dark purple tulips flower in the wall border. Neatly clipped topiary birds signal the entrance to the Bathing Pool Garden.

41

16 THE BATHING POOL GARDEN

The yew hedge dominates the garden with its strictly Palladian portico surmounting the semi-circular flight of steps to the quiet roundel beyond. The area is restrained in its planting. Fine shuttlecock ferns (*Matteuccia struthiopteris*) and skunk cabbage flourish under the big magnolia, *M. × soulangeana*. In the courtyard with its thatched loggia, big pots contain stag's horn sumachs (*Rhus typhina laciniata*) and blue-leaved hostas.

17 THE POPPY GARDEN

Hostas (the narrow-leaved *H. lancifolia* and *H. ventricosa*) mixed with hellebores make a thick carpet under tall specimens of *Hydrangea villosa* and the strange pink bracts hanging from *Cornus florida rubra*. Blue camassias poke through the undergrowth in early May. The narrow curving path of creamy stone set on edge is particularly pleasing, flanked bossily by the foliage of the hostas.

18–21 THE STREAM GARDEN

In contrast with the severely geometric layout of the rest of the garden, the Stream Garden, a large area lying either side of the Long Walk, is charmingly informal. Meandering paths take you along the stream or across to Westonbirt or up to Mrs Winthrop's Garden. From the lower part of the Stream Garden, you can wander in a wide loop back to the rock bank by the Pillar Garden. It is perhaps at its best in spring, with clouds of blue-flowered brunnera, trilliums, the vivid yellow spathes of skunk lily and some elegant stands of fern. The texture of the paths made from creamy local stone is exactly right for this area. They are not the easiest to walk on, but nothing else would do as well.

Blue-flowered comfrey hugs the stream bank in the Lower Stream Garden, where ground cover jostles under the shrubs. Epimediums give way to the handsome leaves of the variegated *Arum italicum pictum*. The architectural bronze foliage of rodgersia (*R. pinnata* 'Superba') spreads like torn umbrellas over primulas and periwinkle. Daffodils and brunnera carpet the ground under a handsome *Magnolia denudata*. Mauve rhododendrons and apricot-orange azaleas flourish in the specially made-up soil along the stream banks. As the azaleas begin to fade, stout magenta primulas take their place.

22 WESTONBIRT

Westonbirt takes its name from the great arboretum near Tetbury, founded in 1829 by Robert Stayner Holford. Johnston was a friend of his son, George. Cherry blossom and the shrimp-pink new foliage of maples are the chief pleasures of this area in April. The most brilliant pink foliage comes from *Acer pseudoplatanus* 'Brilliantissimum'. Before leaves begin fully to camouflage the trees, you can give the handsome bark of the birches and the maples the attention it deserves. *Acer griseum* has bark that peels in cinnamon strips from the trunk. *Acer grosseri hersii* has bark striped green and white, like a snake. The

(*Opposite*) The box-edged borders of the Fuchsia Garden are planted with blue scillas in spring. Topiary birds flank the entrance to the Bathing Pool Garden beyond

(*Right*) Candelabra primulas in the Stream Garden, with a view into Westonbirt beyond (May)

flat-topped cherry with wide-spreading branches and clusters of double white flowers is *Prunus* 'Shimidsu-zakura'.

23 THE SPRING SLOPE

The effect here is wild, naturalistic and the area is at its best in April and May with sheets of starry blue periwinkle (*Vinca major* 'Oxyloba'), white and pale blue wood anemones, white honesty, Solomon's seal, daffodils, and, later, tall white camassias. Hellebores, as always, provide strong clumps of foliage under the groves of young birch.

24 THE ROCK BANK

This long mound of rock and scree is planted to give a Mediterranean effect. Various small conifers (*Juniperus communis* 'Hibernica', *Juniperus × media* 'Pfitzeriana', *Pinus densiflora* 'Umbraculifera'), rosemary and the rock rose, *Cistus × corbariensis*, provide an evergreen setting for more ephemeral displays such as the brilliant lime green mounds of *Valeriana phu* 'Aurea'. Near the top of the mound on its western edge, a grove of gaunt-stemmed *Aralia elata*, the angelica tree, breaks into leaf by the beginning of May. The Golden Rose of China, *R. hugonis*, introduced into this country only eight years before Johnston came to Hidcote, is by May already covered in pale primrose yellow flowers. The rose 'Hidcote Gold' is equally early, but has brighter yellow flowers and broader, wedge-shaped thorns on its stems. Both roses have attractive ferny foliage.

By the end of May, pale white, cream and pink brooms are flowering on the Rock Bank with mats of perennial wallflower in shades of mauve and orange. Yellow and white potentillas are draped over the rocks with grey-leaved dorycnium and the dwarf *Hebe pinguifolia* 'Pagei'. A navelwort, *Omphalodes cappadocica* from Turkey, spreads mats of bright azure blue flowers over the bank in May.

25 THE CAMELLIA CORNER

A narrow entrance gap in the hedge leads from the Theatre Lawn into this dark-leaved corner with the yew-like *Cephalotaxus harringtonia* on the right and the drooping needle foliage of *Juniperus recurva coxii* on the left. Purple honesty seeds itself about happily in the deep shade.

26 THE PINE GARDEN

Pale pink cistus and the double yellow helianthemum 'Jubilee' fill the small raised circular bed. Handsome Portugal laurels clipped into domes have replaced the standard bay trees that stood here in Johnston's time. The laurels, being hardy, are easier to manage. The pool has low mounds of grey foliage around it and, in early May, the beautiful acid yellow blooms of *Paeonia mlokosewitschii*. By the end of May huge spiky agaves are brought out from their winter shelters and set in pots round the pool. Beyond the pool is a mixed shrub border which includes the double magenta-flowered rose, *R. rugosa* 'Roseraie de l'Hay'.

27 THE ROSE BORDERS

Either side of the entrance are clumps of *Viburnum rhytidophyllum* with handsome, evergreen leaves, the undersides covered with a buff-coloured down. Tall pillars of Irish yew provide a backdrop for the

The Rose Borders in May, when lilacs and standard wistaria are among the principal features

borders which will later be filled with the smell of roses. In spring you will find narcissus, auriculas and blue grape hyacinths in drifts between the low-spreading mats of purple-leaved sage. At the beginning of May tall lilacs fitted in between the Irish yew come into flower. The single dark reddish purple variety is *Syringa* 'Souvenir de Louis Spaeth'. 'Capitaine Baltet' is a single pale lilac and the graceful single white variety is 'Vestale'. The long racemes of the standard wistarias planted either side of the seat at the end of the path are flowering by the end of May with tall alliums and yellow asphodels in the borders, together with mauve and white lupins. At the end of May too, the first roses start to bloom. Look out for the pale pink rugosa 'Fru Dagmar Hastrup' and the famous old 'Fantin-Latour' on the left-hand side, heavily double pale pink blooms with a smell that sends you reeling.

28 THE KITCHEN GARDEN

During the Second World War Hidcote supplied four hospitals with produce from this vast area, but it is not run as a kitchen garden any longer. When the Trust first took over at Hidcote, shrubs for sale were propagated and grown on here. Now masses of spare plants for the garden are lined out in beds separated by paths and old espalier fruit trees. A new orchard has been planted at the far end. The frameyard and greenhouses are not open to visitors.

Summer

1 THE COURTYARD

Even in the height of summer, strong foliage remains one of the great pleasures of this courtyard: the handsome leaves of *Magnolia delavayi* and gaunt *Mahonia lomariifolia* in the corner to the right of the ticket office, the spiky grey foliage of *Kniphofia caulescens* to the left of the garden entrance. By June the purple potato flower (*Solanum crispum* 'Glasnevin') has started a display that continues all summer and the huge bush of *Cotoneaster glaucophyllus serotinus* is humming with the sound of bees.

The smell of mock orange hangs in the air, drowning the fainter scent of the dark violet-purple rambler rose 'Violette' climbing up the gatepost by the far entrance. By July schizophragma is flowering against the wall of the small chapel. It looks very like a climbing hydrangea, but the bracts are spoon-shaped round the central cluster of flowers. Lavender 'Hidcote' and the purple hebe 'Autumn Glory' flower at its feet.

By July too, the special 'Hidcote' hypericum will be in flower behind the grey leaves of the kniphofia and the first flowers will be showing on the hydrangeas and fuchsias. Replacing the rose on the gate pillar is the well-known fuchsia 'Mrs Popple' and a pale pink-flowered version of the wild *Fuchsia magellanica*. To the right of the ticket office is the pale pink lacecap *Hydrangea macrophylla* 'Lilacina' and to the left the elegant white 'Veitchii'.

2 THE GARDEN YARD

Fuchsias and geraniums replace the earlier-flowering hyacinths and tulips in the tubs. The fuchsia with pale stamens, pink bell and white upswept sepals is 'Hidcote Beauty'. The lead tank is planted with heliotrope and grey helichrysum.

3 THE THEATRE LAWN

If you look back from the big beech across this lawn, you get one of the few glimpses of the outside world that the garden allows. Otherwise you have to walk to the very perimeter, at the end of the Long Walk or beyond the hornbeam stilts, to catch the wider view. The yew hedges round the lawn are grand and formal, but the hedge that stretches down from the restaurant beside the path has been patched at the bottom with box, which gives quite a different texture.

4 THE OLD GARDEN

Old mushroom-like staddle-stones (traditionally used to support hay ricks) make the path here, the rhomboid shapes of the bases contrasting with the rounds of the tops. A steep step leads down from the entrance through the narrow doorway, one of the

The Theatre Lawn

many changes of level in the garden. The colour scheme in the two main borders centres round soft blues and pinks. Tall clumps of *Iris monspur* 'Cambridge Blue' provide good foliage as well as thin fleur-de-lis flowers, pale blue with yellow throats. The borders are not matched, though some plants – the iris, *Rosa glauca*, grey pools of lamb's ear – are repeated on both sides. Anchusa, brilliant magenta mounds of *Geranium psilostemon*, campanulas (*C. latiloba* 'Hidcote Amethyst', *C. lactiflora* 'Loddon Anna', *C. latifolia*), astrantia and the purple-smudged flowers of *Philadelphus* 'Belle Etoile' dominate the June border, with, towards the end of the month, big bushes of hybrid musk roses such as the rich pink 'Felicia'.

By July the low-growing pink floribunda rose 'Nathalie Nypels' raised in Holland in 1919 starts a display which continues the whole of the summer. Tender plants, such as salvias, argyranthemums, felicias and osteospermums, settle into the gaps left by the earlier-flowering tulips. In the side border on the left-hand side, tall wands of azure blue *Salvia uliginosa*, coaxed on in the greenhouse, are already leaning over phlox (*P. paniculata* 'Alba') and big white shasta daisies. White hydrangeas (*H. arborescens* 'Grandiflora') fill the wooden tubs that line the side path. Johnston had tender pomegranates here. There are sprawling mounds of the herbaceous clematis, *C. integrifolia* 'Hendersonii', with nodding blue flowers standing on long stems above the foliage. Under the cedar is a sea of purple-leaved *Viola labradorica*, pink oxalis and grey *Artemisia* 'Powis Castle'.

The centre borders are dominated by exotic-looking tall pink salvias (*S. involucrata* 'Bethellii' and 'Boutin'), until at the end of July the dahlias begin to flower. These are a great feature of the Old Garden in the second half of summer and bloom until the first frosts stop them in their tracks. The very tall dark purple one is 'Admiral Rawlings', the pale one with mauve staining the edges of the petals is 'Eveline', the pink 'Gerrie Hoek'. The semi-tender argyranthemums take a little while to get into their stride too, but in July the pink powder-puff flowers of 'Mary Wootton' are mingling with the pale blue heads of *Viola cornuta*. The pale yellow *Osteospermum* 'Buttermilk' provides a gentle contrast with clumps of pale apricot day lilies. In the foreground, near the entrance from the Circle, a superb grass, *Pennisetum orientale*, comes into flower, with feathery grey-pink heads like the hairiest kind of caterpillar. Blue-flowered felicias are also best suited to the front of a border. In the Old Garden their bright blue daisy flowers contrast well with the pink 'Nathalie Nypels' rose.

By the end of July tall clumps of white goat's rue (*Galega officinalis* 'Alba') fill the narrow side border where they contrast with the brilliant blue-hooded flowers of *Salvia patens*. Sprawling plants of the white *Clematis viticella* 'Alba Luxurians' are used as ground cover. Clouds of *Gypsophila paniculata* make a foil for the deep purple flowers of the heliotrope bedded out here, and a low-growing *Gypsophila* 'Rosy Veil' fills the space in front of the bright blue-flowered *Clematis* × *durandii*.

In the double borders *Yucca flaccida* comes into flower. This is a particularly graceful species, with narrow, greyish leaves, drooping at the tips. Tall spikes of brilliant blue salvias contrast well with white cactus dahlias. Penstemons come into their own in August, white penstemon with the dwarf mauve *Aster* × *thompsonii* 'Nana' and mounds of pink argyranthemum. In August, though, nothing can compete with the exuberance of the dahlias,

Bird topiary, 'Gruss an Aachen' roses and campanula in the White Garden (June)

here cleverly buttressed and staked against the weather. White cactus dahlias ('My Love') jostle clumps of *Aster × frikartii*, the best of the Michaelmas daisies with big shaggy flowers of mauve, yellow-centred. Pink dahlias overpower the elegant Japanese anemones. You can't adjust the volume on dahlias, though. They sing *fortissimo* or not at all.

The narrow borders underneath the cottage at the far right-hand edge of the Old Garden run by way of a gravel and stone path to the back of the Maple Garden. The border under the wall was specially made up with lime-free soil to grow rhododendrons and other calcifuge shrubs. By June the blue Himalayan poppies (*Meconopsis × sheldonii*) are just finishing, but there are enchanting small orchid-like roscoeas and *Allium sphaerocephalon*. Later in the summer you may see white agapanthus and the handsome foliage of *Francoa sonchifolia*. Fluffy purple heads appear on top of the tall dark stems of *Eupatorium purpureum*, together with greenish-white spires from *Veratrum album*.

5 THE WHITE GARDEN

A path of small, formal square paving-stones leads from the Old Garden into the White Garden with its stylised topiary birds. They are not all the same. On the right-hand side the birds have tails at right angles to their bodies. On the left, the tails curl over like squirrels. There are curves everywhere here: on the tops of the topiary arches over the hedge openings, in the balusters of box leading to the cedar lawn and the drums on which the birds sit. By June the tall block of holly is dribbling with the red flame flower, *Tropaeolum speciosum*. When it needs trimming, it takes the gardeners a whole day to put up the scaffolding round this holly bush and another eight man-hours to clip the ball on top.

In June the great mounds of crambe are just coming into flower like huge cow parsleys. There are white Canterbury bells and a very pale, low-growing floribunda rose 'Gruss an Aachen', creamy white flowers overlaid with soft pink. It was raised in Germany, just two years after Johnston came to Hidcote, and flowers throughout the summer. *Lamium* 'White Nancy' and *Artemisia* 'Lambrook Silver' are used as ground cover.

A little white-flowered feverfew (*Tanacetum parthenium* 'White Bonnet') gives a pleasantly cottagey feeling to the planting here, with low-growing grey-leaved *Anaphalis triplinervis*. Later there are white phlox and osteospermums with tall sweetly scented white nicotianas and the pale variegated leaves of *Fuchsia magellanica molinae*.

6 THE MAPLE GARDEN

The vista through from the Maple Garden to the far end of the Old Garden is accentuated by the use of the same Regency-style iron seats at either end. Maples are thin on the ground now, as four were lost during recent dry summers. But the one by the seat, a type of *Acer palmatum dissectum*, is superb. And the shape of this garden is pleasing with its two raised beds either side, the shapes curving like the apse of a church. The spring hyacinths in the centre beds have been replaced by formal blocks of heliotrope, with lines of silver artemisia down the centre. Vivid mounds of magenta-flowered *Geranium psilostemon* dominate the raised beds either side. There is a big specimen of the lacecap hydrangea 'Lanarth White' on the left-hand side of the path that leads out of the Maple Garden at the back. The other pale hydrangea with heads starting pale green, turning to cream is *H. arborescens discolor* 'Sterilis'. The tall plume of variegated foliage comes from the holly *Ilex aquifolium* 'Argentea Marginata'. In June look out for the rambling rose 'Paul's Himalayan Musk' tumbling out of the yew tree on the left-hand side of the path by the stream.

7 THE CIRCLE

After its explosion of lilac blossom in spring, the Circle is quiet, just a few Welsh poppies (*Meconopsis cambrica*) drifting on into summer with *Geranium renardii* and a compact form of alchemilla, *A. conjuncta*. In design terms the Circle is vital. It acts as a pivot between two arms of the garden. As one looks west from the Circle, the view stretches between the dramatic Red Borders, through the hornbeam stilts and out through the gates at the end of the garden. Looking south, a much narrower vista carries you through the Fuchsia Garden, over the Bathing Pool

The north Red Border (August)

and into the corresponding green circle at the extreme edge of the garden. The grass circle with its brick paving is certainly circular, but the boundaries are not. We just assume that they must be, camouflaged as they are by the tall growth of the lilacs. The boundaries are borrowed from other areas: wide-leaved holly mixed with copper beech in front of the Red Borders, to introduce us to the colour theme to come, yew on the side that abuts the Theatre Lawn, fancy ironwork at the entrance to the Old Garden. The plain grass circle in the centre has to work hard to overcome the disparate elements and uneven parameters of the boundary.

8 THE RED BORDERS

These borders get dressed for summer at the beginning of June, when huge wheelbarrow loads of cannas and lobelias and other exotica are brought down from their shelters in the Kitchen Garden and planted out amongst the permanent inhabitants of the border: purple-leaved nut and sycamore, purple-leaved cherries, including *Prunus cerasifera* 'Pissardii' and the surprising *Pinus mugo*. The cordylines are plunged in their pots but the cannas, dahlias, verbenas and lobelias are bedded out. When they are lifted in the autumn, the clumps of cannas and lobelias are split up. They are replanted in ten-inch pots and overwintered under glass.

With the poppies and the tulips finished, dark foliage dominates the border, with mounds of

Wall   **Yew hedge**

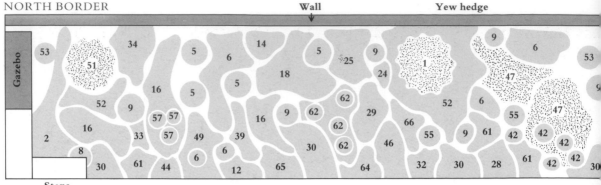

Steps

1 *Acer platanoides* 'Crimson King'
2 *Aconitum* 'Spark's Variety'
3 *Ajuga reptans* 'Atropurpurea'
4 *Begonia* 'Hatton Castle'
5 *Buddleja* 'Black Knight'
6 *Canna indica* 'Le Roi Humbert'
7 *Cimicifuga racemosa*
8 *Clematis viticella* 'Kermesina'
9 *Cordyline australis purpurea*
10 *Cordyline australis purpurea*
    (narrow leaf form)
11 *Corylus maxima* 'Purpurea'
12 *Cosmos atrosanguineus*
13 *Cotinus atropurpureus*
14 *Crocosmia* 'Lucifer'
15 *Dahlia* 'Alva's Doris'
16 *D.* 'Bishop of Llandaff'
17 *D.* 'Bloodstone'
18 *D.* 'Doris Day'
19 *D.* 'Grenadier'
20 *D.* 'Kochelsee'
21 *D.* 'Red Diamond'
22 *D.* 'Red Pygmy'
23 *D.* 'Yvonne'
24 *Delphinium* 'Startling'

25 *Fuchsia fulgens*
26 *F.* 'Rufus'
27 *Geum* 'Borisii'
28 *Hebe* 'Amy'
29 *Hemerocallis* 'Alan'
30 *H. fulva*
    'Kwanso Flore Pleno'
31 *H.* 'Stafford'
32 *Heuchera* 'Palace Purple'
33 *Kniphofia uvaria*
34 *Lilium pardalinum*
35 *Lobelia cardinalis*
    'Bees Flame'
36 *L. card.* 'Cherry Ripe'
37 *L. card.* 'Queen Victoria'
38 *L. card.* 'Will Scarlet'
39 *Miscanthus sinensis*
    'Gracillimus'
40 *Papaver*
    'Beauty of Livermere'
41 *P.* 'May Queen'
42 *Pelargonium* 'Generale
    Championette'
43 *P.* 'Henry Jacoby'
44 *Penstemon* 'Schoenholzeri'

45 *Phlox* 'Prince of Orange'
46 *Phormium tenax*
47 *Pinus mugo* with *Clematis*
    'Viticella Rubra'
48 *Polygonum amplexicaule*
49 *Potentilla* 'Gibson's Scarlet'
50 *Prunus cerasifera* 'Pissardii'
51 *P. spinosa* 'Purpurea'
52 *Pulmonaria saccharata*
53 *Rheum palmatum* 'Atrosanguineum'
54 *Rosa* 'Evelyn Fison'
55 *R.* 'Frensham'
56 *R.* 'Josephine Bruce,
    Climbing'
57 *R.* 'Marlena'
58 *R. moyesii* 'Geranium'
59 *R.* 'Orange Triumph'
60 *R.* 'Super Star'
61 *Salvia elegans*
62 *S. fulgens*
63 *S. microphylla neurepia*
64 *S. officinalis atropurpurea*
65 *Verbena* 'Huntsman'
66 *V.* 'Lawrence Johnston'
67 *Viola labradorica*

Trellis fence

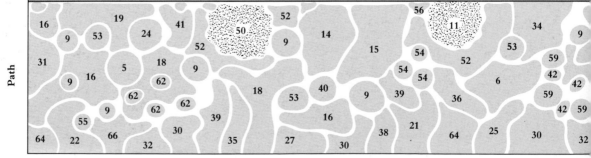

Path

SOUTH BORDER

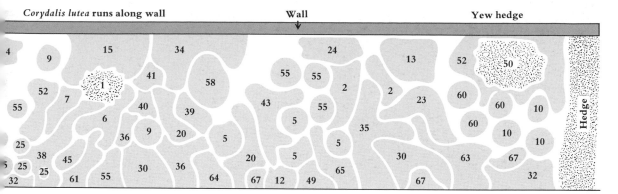

Corydalis lutea runs along wall   **Wall**   **Yew hedge**

purple sage, carpets of dark bugle and regular clumps of *Heuchera micrantha*, its dark green leaves flushed with bronze. By the end of the month the well-known floribunda rose 'Frensham' is adding splashes of pure red, and huge panther lilies (*L. pardalinum*), up to seven feet high, crane over bronze explosions of cordyline. A haze of buff flower surrounds the heavy bulk of purple-leaved cotinus. Dark blue delphiniums slotted in along the back of the border make the contrasting reds seem even redder.

These borders are at their most sumptuous by late July. Then, all the tender plants bedded out at the beginning of June are beginning to flower and the bold clumps of double orange day lilies (*Hemerocallis fulva* 'Kwanso Flore Pleno') used at intervals in the foreground of both borders are in full flow. The lobelias, used much more in Edwardian gardens than they are in modern ones, are stunning. The green-leaved variety is 'Cherry Ripe'. The others, 'Bees Flame' and 'Will Scarlet', have purple leaves. Red dahlias have begun their display too, but they come on strongest when the lobelias start to fade.

'Bishop of Llandaff' dahlia pays rent twice in this border, for its handsome bronze foliage has its own beauty long before the brilliant single red flowers begin to appear. 'Grenadier' has foliage that is almost as good, setting off its double red flowers. Other dahlias used here are 'Bloodstone', the medium decorative variety 'Red Diamond' and the small cactus varieties 'Alva's Doris' and 'Doris Day'. The miniature decorative variety 'Kochelsee' is a recent addition.

Tender fuchsias and salvias need time to build up to their best performance too, so wait until late July or August to see rich *Salvia fulgens*, the Cardinal Sage introduced from Mexico at the beginning of the nineteenth century. It grows to about three feet with lush foliage and lippy flowers of traffic light red. Its cousin, *S. microphylla neurepia*, came from Mexico at the same time but is bigger, with equally vivid flowers. The fuchsias are mostly types of *F. fulgens*, such as 'Rufus', with lush, dark foliage and long, thin tubular flowers, orange-red rather than purplish.

The most lustrous effect comes from the cannas,

Trellis fence

Steps

especially when sunlight shines through their huge paddle-shaped leaves. Only faithful brigades in Parks Departments all over the country kept these magnificently tropical-looking plants from disappearing altogether, after they had fallen out of favour in private gardens. The variety used at Hidcote is 'Le Roi Humbert'. They have tubers like a dahlia's and are equally irresistible to slugs when the new foliage first unfurls from the base. The flowers are like flames.

9 THE STILT GARDEN

The Stilt Garden, a very French idea, and the gazebos were added after 1915. There would have been a lot of earth moving to do here, for the ground rises steeply from the Red Borders. Turning to look through the gazebo doors along the Long Walk, you realise how steeply the land falls away here too. The beds at the end are edged with yew rather than box, with fountains of pampas foliage and the bloodless flowers of Vatican sage, *Salvia sclarea turkestanica*. In each bed is a paulownia, pruned heavily at regular intervals to stimulate a supply of large fresh leaves. The equally large leaves of the vine *Vitis coignetiae* sprawl over the margins of the right-hand bed. Anchusas ('Loddon Royalist') dominate the beds in June with the yellow spires of self-sown verbascum. In August the gardeners begin the exacting task of trimming the hornbeam hedges in the Stilt Garden. It is all done by eye. Scaffolding, built like a siege tower, gives them at least a firm footing.

10 THE PILLAR GARDEN

The yew pillars dominate this area, poised as if for some stately court dance, advancing towards each other across the central grass lawn, then retreating to their solid square bases to pose until the next visitor has disappeared. It is laid out in a series of parallel paths and beds with mock orange scenting the air in June. These are planted at the top, next to the boundary hedge, *Philadelphus* 'Belle Etoile' with smudgy mauve centres in its abundant creamy white flowers, 'Beauclerk' with a less pronounced mauve stain. When the philadelphus has finished,

the huge stands of *Romneya coulteri* come into flower, white tissue paper poppy heads springing from handsome grey foliage. Hedges of lavender line the narrow path and release a different, more pungent fragrance as you brush by them. The peonies, so stunning in May, have completely finished, but you may still catch the faded drumstick heads of the alliums that grow behind them.

On the lower level agapanthus are the stars by late July and continue to look stunning for most of August. Behind them are fuchsias (*F.* 'Margaret', 'Baby Blue Eyes', 'Thompsonii' and 'Kwintet') and, springing between the yew pillars, 'Hidcote' lavender. The bottom right-hand corner of this garden flames with brilliant orange *Alstroemeria aurantiaca*, a native of southern Chile, set against the equally

Fuchsias and agapanthus in the Pillar Garden (August)

brilliant yellow of a broom, *Spartium junceum*. More fuel is added to the fire with blazing 'Harlequin' hybrid lilies.

The two big beds below the Pillar Garden are in transition. Formerly this was a phlox garden, but eelworm got the better of most of the phlox. Two newly planted rows of upright hawthorns (*Crataegus oxyacantha* 'Erectus') replace 'Amanogawa' cherries on the left-hand side, by the double row of peonies. The rest has yet to find an identity, though white Jacob's ladder (*Polemonium caeruleum album*), the ever-willing herbaceous geranium 'Buxton's Variety' and masses of lilies plunged in pots, make a colourful mosaic.

11 THE TERRACE

Huge mounds of *Hebe rakaiensis*, like heavyweights all on one side of a seesaw, weigh down the western end of the terrace. The leaf is neat, pale green. The flowers, which come in June, are carried in small white spikes. At the other end, by the pavilions, a magnificent *Cytisus battandieri* with silky grey foliage fills the air in June with its pineapple scent. Pale potentillas, the white-flowered *P. davurica veitchii* with a greyish sheen on the leaves, and the similar 'Farrer's White' continue to give a gentle display all summer supported by the neat foliage of various pinks. The best grey foliage comes from clumps of hawkweed (*Hieracium waldsteinii*).

12 THE WINTER BORDER

The background to this is the square-patterned wooden trellis that divides it from the Red Borders behind, and it occasionally borrows stray visitors from this border for its own. In June you can find clumps of the unusual yellow-flowered gentian, *G. lutea*, growing here. Thalictrum thrives under the big magnolia and by August there are sheets of *Strobilanthes atropurpureus*. This is a plant better seen in the morning than the afternoon, for the flowers, a gorgeous blue when they first come out, fade to a less attractive purple as they age. Opposite the Winter Border is a magnificent cut-leaf elder (*Sambucus laciniata*), by August weighed down with huge flat bunches of berries. Opposite too is an

inviting cool tunnel of pleached limes. A mosaic of shadows patterns the ground when the sun shines through it.

13 THE LONG WALK

'Was it fortuitous that all the long, formal views, ending in an open invitation to explore further, were arranged on ground rising before one?' wrote Graham Stuart Thomas in the 1979 edition of *Gardens of the National Trust*. 'The irresistible urge is in everyone to mount each slope . . .: a journey ever upwards with the reward at the top.' Manipulating Hidcote's odd site, which slopes in several directions, was a major challenge to the ingenuity of its owner. The smooth lines of the hornbeam hedge become like stage flats, with us, the garden visitors, as the actors, making our entrances and exits across the wide stage of grass, from Westonbirt to the Stream Garden, from the Stream Garden to the Pillar Garden.

14 MRS WINTHROP'S GARDEN

Blue and yellow flowers continue the theme that was started in spring with golden creeping Jenny and blue pansies. The creeping Jenny (*Lysimachia nummularia* 'Aurea') continues to spread over the low central beds, eventually dripping over the edges like custard over a tart. In June yellow alliums (*A. moly*) poke out of the carpet. By late July dwarf blue *Agapanthus* 'Lilliput' have replaced them. A froth of alchemilla lines the paths at the top end of the garden until it is sheared down in August. The same greeny-yellow flowers appear on tall stands of *Thalictrum speciosissimum*, which has finely cut leaves of steely blue-green. There are tall euphorbias, yellow Turk's cap lilies and brilliant blue anchusas in June, with a paler blue coming from the powder-puff flowers of *Ceanothus* 'Henri Desfossé'. On the brick plinths stand pots of bronze cordyline and variegated agaves.

Mounds of *Hypericum* 'Hidcote' light up the ground underneath the rustling *Trachycarpus* palms. Tall dark blue monkshoods (*Aconitum napellus*) stand in blocks either side of the exit to the Stream Garden. By July the exuberant golden hops in the corners have left their tripods and are clambering over the copper beech hedge.

15 THE FUCHSIA GARDEN

Because the central design is kept so low – a parterre of box-edged beds filled with dwarf fuchsias – you are perhaps more conscious here than anywhere else of the beauty of Hidcote's hedges: intricate tapestries of copper beech, hollies, box and yew. Between the Fuchsia Garden and the Bathing Pool Garden is a box hedge, about four feet high with yew birds facing each other over the steps down to the pool.

The variegated fuchsia, *F. magellanica* 'Variegata', makes a good foliage feature in the central oval before it ever comes into flower. The bushy dwarf fuchsia 'Tom Thumb', raised in France in the 1850s, is used in the right-hand triangular beds, the paler 'Lady Thumb' in the left-hand beds. 'Cupid'

climbs over the brick wall, a rose with large peach-pink single flowers, each with a central boss of golden stamens. It was raised by the rose firm Cants in 1915. At the back, the brick path disappears entirely under a Mediterranean-looking evergreen, *Pittosporum dallii*.

16 THE BATHING POOL GARDEN

'Iceberg' roses grow either side of the steps down to this garden with a spreading *Magnolia × soulangeana* on the left-hand side, underplanted with a quiet, elegant colony of shuttlecock ferns. Wild-looking *Corydalis ochroleuca* with white flowers and filigree foliage hang out of the retaining wall at the back. In front is a narrow curving border, home first to hairy-leaved meconopsis, then wands of blue-flowered willow gentian, *G. asclepiadea*, followed in late August by the magnificent spires of white bottle brush flowers on *Cimicifuga racemosa*. At the far end, steps rise to the third circle in the line from the one beyond the Fuchsia Garden. Looking back that way, you see tiers of hedges rising parallel to one another, the low hedge of box in the Fuchsia Garden surmounted by the mixed hedge of beech and holly behind, with the yew hedge of the Theatre Lawn on top of that.

The small courtyard that leads off the Bathing Pool Garden is paved in red tiles that look too much like a kitchen floor to be entirely successful. Johnston did not spend money on the construction of his paths, paving and walls. Materials were mostly re-used from other parts of the house and garden and the steps and walls were built without proper foundations. But this is a pleasant, contemplative place to sit on hot days. Big *Hosta sieboldiana* grow in terracotta pots here, together with a matching pair of stag's horn sumachs (*Rhus typhina*), which have to be replaced at regular intervals when they have grown too leggy. Pink bleeding heart and splendid ferns enjoy cool billets at the feet of the walls.

(*Left*) Dwarf fuchsia 'Tom Thumb' in the Fuchsia Garden (August)

17 THE POPPY GARDEN

Not so much poppies as hostas, which have spread to make an almost unbroken carpet under hydrangeas, which are at their best from late July. Then both the hostas and the magnificent *Hydrangea villosa* are in flower. Swags of the huge-leaved *Vitis coignetiae* sprawl over the arch from the courtyard.

18–21 THE STREAM GARDEN

This is a large and rambling area, made up from four geographically distinct locations. First, there is the area immediately outside the plain green circle into which the path from the Poppy Garden leads. The upper path here takes you to the bog garden and then to Westonbirt, but if you take the first narrow path to the right, it leads past a huge evergreen *Osmanthus forrestii*, with cool slabs of rock underneath, lacy fronds of maidenhair fern (*Adiantum venustum*) and moss, as cool and elegant a combination as you would find in any Japanese garden. This path hugs the boundary of the Bathing Pool Garden to bring you over the stream to a rather indeterminate area east of Mrs Winthrop's Garden. In late August *Kirengeshoma palmata* with shiny black stems and shuttlecock flowers of palest lemon yellow thrives in a corner by the path from the Bathing Pool Garden. In its season, it is the most beautiful thing in the Stream Garden.

Immediately below Mrs Winthrop's Garden is a different part of the Stream Garden. At the top is a newly planted area with *Polygonum* 'Superbum', yellow-flowered *Crocosmia* 'Solfaterre', francoa, perovskia and white lacecap hydrangeas. From here the ground slopes steeply down to the stream which is bordered with huge blocks of hosta and several kinds of ligularia, all of which enjoy the damp conditions here. *L. przewalskii* has black stems, jagged leaves and spires of yellow flowers. Juicy spikes of terracotta flowers, the texture of plush, rise from clumps of rodgersia. They are particularly good contrasted with the rounded blue leaves of hosta and the rich dark blue flowers of tradescantia.

(Right) The stone path through the Lower Stream Garden is lined with lush foliage in summer

By July plumes of astilbe flowers in pink and deep red rise between the bulky foliage of the skunk cabbage and brunnera. A tall wild-looking phlox, the original *P. paniculata*, billows in a stately fashion in front of the huge mauve panicles on *Hydrangea sargentiana*, and white lacecap hydrangeas.

On the far side of the Long Walk is another extensive area of the Stream Garden with a path wandering along the left-hand bank of the little stream to a bridge and an open glade beyond. *Ligularia dentata* 'Desdemona' has rounded dark, almost purple leaves with flaming orange flowers. A superb Indian horse chestnut (*Aesculus indica*) grows by the bridge. It has candelabra flowers of pink in June. Another path loops back over the higher ground bordering the Long Walk. Ligularias shine out here in June, with ferns erupting amongst them. Pale acid yellow flag irises rise from the stream bed, contrasting with martagon lilies and the

last of the magenta primulas. Epimediums, white woodruff and *Ranunculus aconitifolius* 'Flore Pleno', a double white buttercup, are used as ground cover under shrubs on the left-hand side. Since the ilex in this area have been cut back heavily, the plants underneath have grown much better. Veratrums flourish, sending up tall white flower spikes in early July.

22 WESTONBIRT

Roses are the surprise in Westonbirt in early summer: 'La Mortola' with greyish foliage and creamy white flowers climbing through a holly, pale pink 'Splendens', the myrrh-scented rose, setting itself at a nothofagus, and the multiflora rambler 'Francis E. Lester', with large trusses of single flowers, white flushed with pink, tackling a pine. There are plenty more. The entrance to Westonbirt is planted with bold, large-leaved herbaceous plants: *Salvia turkestanica*, cimicifuga, hostas, ligularia. By the beginning of August hydrangeas are the most mouth-watering things here, especially the lanky, loose-limbed *Hydrangea aspera macrophylla*, with large flat heads of mauve sterile bracts surrounding a central boss of tightly packed bobble flowers. There is a surprising view from the far side of the bog garden back towards Mrs Winthrop's Garden, nearer than you thought it could be.

23 THE SPRING SLOPE

This is very pretty still at the beginning of summer with stands of wild-looking campanulas, white and blue. The campanulas carry this area right through until the middle of July, together with fine clumps of martagon lilies. After this, its season is over.

24 THE ROCK BANK

A huge macrocarpa used to shade the Rock Bank, making it rather a dark, dingy area. Since that was removed, the bank has been replanted to give a Mediterranean effect with plants that thrive in hot, dry situations. *Cistus* × *corbariensis* and the pale yellow helianthemum 'Wisley Primrose' cover the

bank on the side nearest the Pillar Garden. Khaki-coloured whipcord hebes grow further down under the low, spreading limbs of a pine, *P. densiflora* 'Umbraculifera'. At the Stilt Garden end of the Rock Bank is a splendid multi-stemmed ilex. How did it get like this? Were a handful of seedling ilexes all planted together here? Or is this a single tree, sat upon in extreme youth by an overweight spaniel?

By the end of July a brilliant blue bed of *Gentiana septemfida* springs up on the far side of the Rock Bank and the tall walking sticks of the aralia come into bloom, flat creamy heads like elderflower. A creeping slate-blue mallow accompanies an equally low-growing evening primrose (*Oenothera missouriensis*) on its journey to the feet of a broom, whose seedpods explode in the summer sun.

25 THE CAMELLIA CORNER

This is a quiet transition area, dominated by the yew-like bulk of *Cephalotaxus harringtonia drupacea* on one side and the drooping, weeping shape of *Juniperus recurva coxii* on the other. This is a tree better seen from a distance than close at hand. In August, look out for the clusters of flowers on *Clerodendrum trichotomum fargesii*. Each tiny flower, scented, white, emerges from a pinkish, winged bladder.

26 THE PINE GARDEN

Like the Rock Bank, this has a distinctly Mediterranean feeling, with the clipped mophead trees, the pool and the pots of spiky agaves. The raised bed is surrounded by pale potentillas and rock roses, with silver-leaved bright yellow gazanias planted out between them. On the far side of the pool, the tall geranium 'Mrs Kendall Clark' fills in under rugosa roses and the arching branches of the rose 'Highdownensis'. This has single light crimson flowers, followed later in the season by handsome flagon-shaped hips. Highdown was the Sussex garden belonging to Sir Frederick Stern, a contemporary of Lawrence Johnston whom he met from time to time at Nymans, the home of another gardening friend, Leonard Messel. By August the far side of the pool is fringed with agapanthus and the pale yellow *Argyranthemum* 'Jamaica Primrose' is smothered with daisy flowers.

The pool itself is surrounded by huge stone troughs with thrifts and sempervivums. The planting round the pool is cool: grey and pale sulphur yellow, coming mostly from cotton lavender, with sea lavender, *Limonium latifolium*, adding clouds of mauve flowers for weeks in late summer. A most unusual berberis, *B. temolaica*, grows here, with lustrous grey leaves, rather than the usual shiny dark green. Clipped Portugal laurels guard the entrance to the small grass court behind this garden. In August pink crinums cluster round the feet of the laurels. The eye-catching variegated bush on the right-hand side of the path that leads to the rose borders is *Euonymus fortunei* 'Silver Queen'.

27 THE ROSE BORDERS

At the entrance to the Rose Borders is a magnificent old robinia, *R. × ambigua* 'Decaisneana', with a bark more furrowed than a bloodhound's forehead. It blossoms in early June with tassels of pink pea-like flowers. The rose garden ahead (but *not* the tarmac path) was Johnston's last innovation at Hidcote, made at the suggestion of his friend Norah Lindsay. Two lines of clipped yew trees mark the back of the borders and they are planted with old French roses: gallicas, damasks, mosses and their kind. During the 1960s both borders were completely replanted. The Head Gardener, George Burrows, and his staff cleaned out half a border a year and then fallowed it for a year to get rid of the perennial weed that infested it, mostly bindweed. The path was widened at the same time and the whole exercise took five years. In 1967 *Gardener's Chronicle* reported the splendour of the new border, the roses fronted with various pinks and pools of purple-leaved sage.

These borders are usually (one has to be cautious, given the vagaries of the British weather) at their best during the last two weeks in June. Few of these roses are repeat-flowering. 'Vivid', a Bourbon rose raised in this country in 1853, occasionally throws out some extra blooms after its main early summer season. The flowers are very bright magenta pink with a swoony smell. The frilly pink rugosa 'Pink

The Rose Borders in summer

Grootendorst' is more reliable in the matter of repeat-flowering as are the other rugosas in this border, such as 'Fru Dagmar Hastrup'.

The gallicas are well represented, with the very old variety 'Surpasse Tout', deep cerise-maroon, paling as it ages. 'Marcel Bourgouin' was bred in France in 1899, semi-double flowers of rich, deep red. 'Sissinghurst Castle', which was discovered growing in Vita Sackville-West's garden, has a semi-double flower, richly scented, with deep maroon petals, backed by a paler pink. 'Tuscany Superb', raised in this country in 1848, has similar dark red flowers and obligingly few thorns. It does not have the pale reverses of 'Sissinghurst Castle'.

One of the best of the damasks is 'St Nicholas', bred by Johnston's friend Bobbie James and named after his own Hidcote-style garden at Richmond in Yorkshire. It is like a glorified wild dog rose, the same soft pink, but doubled. The foliage is vigorous and downy grey. Unusually for a damask, it is repeat-flowering. 'Mme Zoetmans', bred in France in 1830, has the palest of pink flowers, very double, each with a neat green eye, like the better known damask 'Mme Hardy'. 'La Ville de Bruxelles' has much richer pink flowers than 'Mme Hardy', but with the same heady perfume characteristic of all the damasks.

The moss roses are particularly appealing and one of the best grown here is 'Mousseux du Japon', very heavily mossed on the buds and even on the stalks of the leaves. The flowers are semi-double, a pale lilac pink. 'Lanei', raised in France in 1854, has dark moss surrounding very double deep crimson flowers, which open flat to show a green eye in the centre. 'A Longues Pedoncules' is named for its long flower stalks, heavily encrusted with moss and holding double flowers of soft pink.

When the roses fade, a wide variety of penstemons come into bloom, 'Garnet', 'Hidcote Pink', 'Sour Grapes' and pale blue 'Alice Hindley'. By the first week in August, most of the colour comes from phlox, with pale-coloured deciduous ceanothus catching up fast. The ceanothus are pruned hard back to two buds each April to keep them a manageable size. At the back of the Rose Border, next to the frames and beds of the Kitchen Garden, is a long border with fine late double peonies and the biennial eryngium, *E. giganteum*, known as 'Miss Willmott's ghost'.

28 THE KITCHEN GARDEN

This was probably the most intensively gardened patch of all in Johnston's day, the headquarters of the gardeners who grew vast amounts of fruit and vegetables, which they sold to local suppliers. Now the area is mostly devoted to raising spare plants for the garden. At the beginning of June, the glasshouse is still full of salvias, geraniums, dahlias, osteospermums, agaves, convolvulus and helichrysum, waiting to move to quarters outside. By July the houses are mostly empty, and the time that has been devoted to looking after them is spent instead on the long summer job of clipping the four and a half miles of hedging in the garden.

Autumn

Frost is the great dictator of the autumn garden. A few nights of sub-zero temperatures in September can bring an early and precipitate end to the stunning performance of the dahlias in the Old Garden and the Red Borders. The team of gardeners start to put the garden's summer clothes – agaves, cordylines, cannas, lobelias and salvias – away in the greenhouses ready for another season. Westonbirt, the large area of trees and shrubs that lies hidden behind the tall hornbeam hedge of the Long Walk, comes into its own with now-or-never displays from the Japanese maples.

1 THE COURTYARD

The huge bush of *Cotoneaster glaucophyllus serotinus* that hummed with bees in summer is, by September, covered with small dusty claret-coloured berries. On the left-hand side of the ticket entrance, fatsia spreads its glossy leaves, topped in October with creamy drumstick heads of flower. The solanum on the other side of the door is still in bloom, with purple potato flowers. By late September *Ceanothus arboreus* 'Trewithen Blue', growing against the chapel and always anxious to beat the clock, will be showing the first of the flowers that it is supposed to save until April. Pink nerines sprout in the narrow border underneath. Lemon-coloured poker flowers with pale buff and apricot tips emerge from the grey whorls of foliage of *Kniphofia caulescens*. Tiny papery cream lanterns hang from the Killarney Strawberry tree, *Arbutus unedo*, a handsome evergreen with a rough brown bark.

2 THE GARDEN YARD

Purple liriope, a useful late-flowering perennial, starts to flower at the beginning of September in the narrow border behind the handkerchief tree, and Japanese anemones flourish amongst the ferns.

3 THE THEATRE LAWN

By late September a few autumn crocuses will be pushing their noses through the grass under the big

The vista from the cedar lawn to the Stilt Garden and the gates on the horizon

beech tree on its dais. The curve of the yew hedge is echoed in the shape of the enclosing yew hedge behind. On the north side a tall avenue of beeches, particularly brilliant in October, leads to curved blue wooden gates and the outside world.

4 THE OLD GARDEN

Provided there are no frosts, autumn continues in an unbroken thread from late summer in the Old Garden. Dahlias are still the most dominant element: the tallest is 'Admiral Rawlings'. There are mounds of the superlative Michaelmas daisy, *Aster* × *frikartii*, and, in the side border, floppy spires of sky blue flowers from *Salvia uliginosa* and shorter spikes from *S. cacaliifolia*, which has bright green wedge-shaped leaves. Cyclamen, first pink shuttlecock flowers, then marbled foliage, fill the dry unpromising bed under the cedar tree. Long bristly

red hips hang from the Chinese rose, *R. setipoda*, in the border under the wooden arch.

5 THE WHITE GARDEN

The white roses 'Gruss an Aachen' give a generous late display, which often continues until October. Though the acanthus spikes begin to fade, the foliage makes huge glossy mounds, an excellent contrast for white flowers around it. White osteospermums are almost at their best and, though the phlox has finished, the grey foliage of *Artemisia* 'Lambrook Silver' continues to look fresh. White bottle-brush flowers top the tall stems of *Cimicifuga ramosa*.

6 THE MAPLE GARDEN

By October the foliage of the drooping maple has turned to a soft bracken colour, though the variegated fuchsias, *F. magellanica* 'Versicolor', continue triumphantly to overflow from the east-facing border. Frost may fell the heliotrope in the central beds but *Knautia macedonica* continues to send up branched stems of crimson-purple pincushion flowers.

7 THE CIRCLE

As the leaves change colour in autumn, the hedges round the Circle change too, the copper beech softening to a foxy brown that stays almost until the new buds of spring. The tapestry hedges, mixtures of yew and box, holly and beech, are one of the great glories of Hidcote. Compare these with what Leyland cypress, the modern hedging favourite, has to offer: no changing colour, no texture, nothing except a galloping propensity to block out the light.

8 THE RED BORDERS

As in the Old Garden, dahlias dominate the borders, glowing against the dark embers of the purple-leaved trees behind. Some of the dahlias, such as 'Bishop of Llandaff' with single red flowers and 'Grenadier' with double, have dark foliage too. In September the tender fuchsias are at their best with lustrous bronzed foliage and long drooping orange-red tube flowers. Some of the roses, such as *R. moyesii*, bear excellent hips, and the brilliant red verbena 'Lawrence Johnston', which grew wild in his French garden at La Serre de la Madone, matches them in the intensity of its colour. Strong upright sheaves of the ornamental grass, *Miscanthus sinensis* 'Gracillimus', by now five feet high, contrast with the symmetrical stiff fountains of cordyline.

9 THE STILT GARDEN

In Johnston's time the pampas grasses *Cortaderia fulvida* were used at regular intervals along the back of the Red Borders. They have been replaced by *Cortaderia selloana* 'Pumila', which is now in full flight here. By October there is a change in colour in the stiff, rough leaves of the vine *Vitis coignetiae* that drapes itself over the low yew hedge of the small enclosures in the Stilt Garden.

10 THE PILLAR GARDEN

Fuchsias hold the stage here during September, particularly the soft mounds of the variegated fuchsia along the top walk, where it is joined by pale pink drifts of flowers on *Abelia* × *grandiflora*. The willing geranium 'Buxton's Variety', blue with a white eye, covers the ground where the summer lilies bloomed. For a curiously tropical view in September, look back from the Long Walk end of the Pillar Garden to the jagged leaves of the aralia on the Rock Bank, silhouetted against the sky, the whole enclosed by a lush, thick backdrop of evergreen ilex trees. By October pink nerines replace the agapanthus in the narrow border by the lawn.

11 THE TERRACE GARDEN

Mounds of pale-leaved *Hebe rakaiensis* continue to dominate the terraces with a scatter of autumn crocus.

12 THE WINTER BORDER

Hips and berries are one of the great joys of the autumn scene at Hidcote. The guelder rose (*Viburnum opulus* 'Compactum') is the star of this border, with bunches of waxy berries replacing its early summer flowers. By October the big vine (*Vitis coignetiae*) draped over the pavilion will be changing colour, its brilliant red and orange echoed in the softer tones of the guelder rose's autumn foliage.

13 THE LONG WALK

All through late summer and autumn the team of Hidcote gardeners will be engaged in trimming the daunting expanse of the hornbeam hedges. From the high land at the end of the vista, you are in a position to see how cleverly Johnston manipulated the sloping ground of the garden into a series of level, roughly south-facing terraces.

The Stilt Garden

14 MRS WINTHROP'S GARDEN

The extremely narrow entrance through the beech hedge into this garden room makes its discovery all the more pleasurable. The dark blue hooded flowers of the monkshoods continue through autumn and the borders of alchemilla in the upper beds refresh themselves with new foliage. Frost can strike early in the Cotswolds and before the end of the season the cordylines and agaves in their pots may have been bundled into the safety of the glasshouse.

15 THE FUCHSIA GARDEN

This is at its best in late summer and autumn when the fuchsias flower at full tilt. The variegated fuchsia is *F. magellanica* 'Variegata'. The smaller beds have the dwarf hybrids 'Tom Thumb' and 'Lady

Thumb'. The hedges at the back and to the right-hand side of this enclosure are particularly intricate with mixes of holly (*Ilex* × *altaclerensis* 'Hodginsii'), yew, copper beech and box.

16 THE BATHING POOL GARDEN

The generous 'Iceberg' roses give a second season of flower here in early autumn, holding their own until the magnificent pampas grass erupts into bloom. Tall bottle-brush flowers of cimicifuga are thrown into sharp relief by the dark background of the yew hedge. Already by the beginning of September the leaves of the stag's horn sumach in the courtyard may be beginning to turn. By October only a few tattered flags will be left. Underneath the magnolia, dark-leaved *Saxifraga fortunei* comes into bloom with lopsided creamy flowers.

17 THE POPPY GARDEN

Until the inevitable collapse of the hostas, these give a wonderfully lush effect, their foliage under-pinning the fading blooms of the hydrangeas. The rough-leaved *Vitis davidii* draped over the entrance from the courtyard gets better and better as the season advances. From the quiet roundel of grass beyond the Poppy Garden you get a beautifully composed view back over the Bathing Pool, past the topiary birds to the mixed hedges beyond.

18–21 THE STREAM GARDEN

There are still new arrivals here: the pale creamy yellow flowers of kirengeshoma borne above the handsome, jagged foliage, the brilliant red flowers of the kaffir lily (*Schizostylis coccinea* 'Major') under the cherry at the entrance to the Lower Stream Garden and the weird spotted purple flowers of the toad lily (*Tricyrtis formosana*). Gentler colour comes from the dying foliage of the big-leaved hostas planted along the stream and from the fading heads of the unusual double-flowered hydrangea, *H. involucrata* 'Hortensis'. The dying fronds of the shuttlecock ferns fan out on the ground like ballet skirts round upright fruiting stems, dark and rough.

22 WESTONBIRT

Tall yellow senecio, white cimicifuga and blue monkshood still bloom in September in the border of large-leaved perennials that you pass coming into Westonbirt from the Long Walk. If you approach directly from the small grass roundel, the wonderful orange and red leaves of a spindle, *Euonymus europaeus*, will be the chief treat. There are ghostly white berries on *Sorbus hupehensis* and waxy yellow clusters on *Viburnum opulus* 'Xanthocarpum'. Bunches of purplish red keys hang from some of the maples, which predominate in this section. You have to wait until October for the full roar of their autumn performance. The berries on the big holly (*Ilex* × *altaclerensis* 'Camelliifolia') are fully ripe by the end of September and glow brilliantly against the glossy evergreen foliage. As you emerge at the top end of Westonbirt, where it gives on to farmland, a sheet of colchicums provides a final surprise.

23 THE SPRING SLOPE

The maple, *Acer palmatum*, against the boundary begins to colour and waxy berries droop from the sober mounds of berberis. If the wind does not find them first, the leaves of the fine Indian horse chestnut, *Aesculus indica*, at the bottom of the slope by the stream turn a foxy burnt orange.

24 THE ROCK BANK

Berries of extraordinary metallic blue are *Viburnum davidii*'s contribution in autumn. The shrub, introduced from western Sichuan in 1904, is handsome at all seasons, with particularly good evergreen leaves, broad and pointed. The veins, running the length of the leaf, are deeply incised. Blue gentians, *G. septemfida* and *G. sino-ornata* 'Kingfisher', flower vividly at the base of the scree.

25 THE CAMELLIA CORNER

The soil at Hidcote is distinctly alkaline, but this is one of several areas in the garden that Johnston treated with huge amounts of sawdust so that he could grow lime-hating shrubs such as camellias.

26 THE PINE GARDEN

The raised circular bed, 'foaming with rock roses of every shade, a lovely surprise, as light as spindrift, shot with many colours the rainbow does not provide', was beautifully brought to life by Vita Sackville-West, writing about Hidcote in 1949. Bright yellow gazanias and potentilla grow there too. By the pool, the generous daisy flowers of *Argyranthemum* 'Jamaica Primrose' contrast beautifully with the stiff formal lines of the agaves in their pots. Tall, swan-necked crinums open their pink trumpet flowers on top of stout, tall stems. Mounds of grey foliage – *Helichrysum microphyllum*, santolina and lavender – soften the straight edges of the lily pool. The Moyesii rose 'Highdownensis', which bore crimson flowers in the summer, now carries equally brilliant hips, flagon-shaped like its parent's.

27 THE ROSE BORDERS

The roses, few of them repeat-flowering, give way to pale blue clouds of ceanothus in September, with wands of caryopteris echoing the gentle misty tones. There are still occasional spikes of flower on the penstemons, though their best season has passed. The orchard behind the Rose Borders is planted with an interesting collection of old varieties of apple. On a still day, the air is full of their complex aromas: the smell of harvest festivals, of autumn.

28 THE KITCHEN GARDEN

Close to the greenhouses, the Japanese honeysuckle (*Leycesteria formosa*) displays quantities of hanging black berries, each topped by dark, beetroot-coloured bracts. By taking out a proportion of the old growth each year, you can ensure a steady new supply of the vivid green stems. As leaves begin to fall, evergreens come into their own. The greenhouses, emptied of their exotic occupants at the beginning of June, now begin to fill up again as frost-tender agaves, cannas and cordylines are brought under cover at the end of their season.

BIBLIOGRAPHY

BROWN, Jane, *Eminent Gardeners*, Viking, London, 1990.

CLARKE, Ethne, *Hidcote: The Making of a Garden*, Michael Joseph, London, 1989.

JEKYLL, Gertrude, and WEAVER, Lawrence, *Gardens for Small Country Houses*, Country Life, London, 1912.

LEES-MILNE, Alvilde, 'Lawrence Johnston, Creator of Hidcote Garden', *National Trust Year Book*, London, 1977–8, pp.18–29.

LEES-MILNE, James, *Ancestral Voices*, Chatto & Windus, London, 1975 [diaries for 1942–3]; *Caves of Ice*, 1983 [1946–7]; *Midway on the Waves*, 1985 [1948–9].

OTTEWILL, David, *The Edwardian Garden*, Yale University Press, London, 1989.

QUEST-RITSON, Charles, *The English Garden Abroad*, Viking, London, 1992, pp.49–52.

RACINE, Michel, et al., *The Gardens of Provence and the French Riviera*, MIT Press, Boston, 1987, pp.280–5.

SACKVILLE-WEST, Vita, 'Hidcote Manor Garden', *Journal of the Royal Horticultural Society*, lxxiv, part 11, November 1949, pp.476–81.

SALES, John, *West Country Gardens*, Alan Sutton, Stroud, 1980, pp.67–71.

THOMAS, Graham Stuart, 'How Past became Present at Hidcote', *The Field*, 19 May 1966.

THOMAS, Graham Stuart, *Gardens of the National Trust*, Weidenfeld & Nicolson, London, 1979, pp.153–6.

TIPPING, H. Avray, 'Hidcote Manor Garden', *Country Life*, lxvii, 1930, pp.286–94; lxviii, 1930, pp.231–3.

WHITSEY, Fred, 'Serre de la Madone', *Country Life*, 10 July 1986, pp.80–1.

The view from Westonbirt into the Stream Garden and Mrs Winthrop's Garden

INDEX